Taking Flight

Inspiration and Techniques to Give Your Creative Spirit Wings

KELLY RAE ROBERTS

NORTH LIGHT BOOKS
CINCINNATI, OHIO

www.mycraftivity.com

Taking Flight. Copyright © 2008 by Kelly Rae Roberts. Manufactured in Singapore. All rights reserved. The written instructions, photographs, designs, patterns and projects in this volume are intended for the personal use of the reader and may be reproduced for that purpose only. Any other use, especially commercial use, is forbidden under law without the express written permission of the copyright holder. Violators will be prosecuted to the fullest extent of the law. No other part of this book may be reproduced in any form or by any electronic or mechanical means including information storage and retrieval systems without permission in writing from the publisher, except by a reviewer, who may quote a brief passage in review. Published by North Light Books, an imprint of F+W Publications, Inc., 4700 East Galbraith Road, Cincinnati, Ohio 45236. (800) 289-0963. First edition.

12 11 10 09 08   5 4 3 2 1

Distributed in Canada by Fraser Direct
100 Armstrong Avenue
Georgetown, ON, Canada L7G 5S4
Tel: (905) 877-4411

Distributed in the U.K. and Europe by David & Charles
Brunel House, Newton Abbot, Devon, TQ12 4PU, England
Tel: (+44) 1626 323200, Fax: (+44) 1626 323319
E-mail: postmaster@davidandcharles.co.uk

Distributed in Australia by Capricorn Link
P.O. Box 704, S. Windsor, NSW 2756 Australia
Tel: (02) 4577-3555

Library of Congress Cataloging-in-Publication Data

Roberts, Kelly Rae,
  Taking flight : inspiration and techniques to give your creative
spirit wings / Kelly Rae Roberts.
    p. cm.
  Includes index.
  ISBN 978-1-60061-082-0
  1. Creative ability. 2. Inspiration. I. Title.
BF408.R515 2008
153.3'5--dc22
                        2008002066

Editor: Jessica Strawser
Designer: Marissa Bowers
Production Coordinator: Greg Nock
Photographers: Ric Deliantoni and Christine Polomsky
Stylist: Jan Nickum

F+W PUBLICATIONS, INC.
www.fwpublications.com

METRIC CONVERSION CHART

TO CONVERT	TO	MULTIPLY BY
Inches	Centimeters	2.54
Centimeters	Inches	0.4
Feet	Centimeters	30.5
Centimeters	Feet	0.03
Yards	Meters	0.9
Meters	Yards	1.1
Sq. Inches	Sq. Centimeters	6.45
Sq. Centimeters	Sq. Inches	0.16
Sq. Feet	Sq. Meters	0.09
Sq. Meters	Sq. Feet	10.8
Sq. Yards	Sq. Meters	0.8
Sq. Meters	Sq. Yards	1.2
Pounds	Kilograms	0.45
Kilograms	Pounds	2.2
Ounces	Grams	28.3
Grams	Ounces	0.035

Dedication

To my husband, John, who knew, well before I did, what I could do. Without a doubt, you have taught me how love unearths the best parts of ourselves.

I'd also like to dedicate this book, and the experience of putting it together, to the spirit of Possibility, how it gracefully enters our lives and gives us a chance to see our own potential. What a remarkable, life-changing thing.

Winged Family, an assemblage by my dear husband, John. It's constructed from an old piece of molding, a vintage doorknob and metal shaped rings.

Gratitude

I have deep, deep gratitude for the people in my life who have encouraged me to discover my own creative spirit. To my mom, whose passion for decorating and whimsy created an early appreciation for all things design, color and fun. Thank you, too, for your unending enthusiasm for me as I made my way into this creative life. To Greggie, for your quiet confidence in me all of these years. You have been a beacon of calm in a sometimes crazy life. To my sister, Jennifer: Your art of poetry, song and gentle assemblages have inspired me beyond words, but none more than your heart. Thank you for your sisterhood, which feels deep and wide. To Tonia, who asked me to write this book: How will I ever express my gratitude to you for birthing a dream I didn't even know I had? There are people who, without ever knowing it, help to change the trajectory of our lives. You are one of those people in my life. To Jessica, my editor extraordinaire, who inspires me to be fun and sassy while still being professional. You do it all and you do it incredibly well, my friend. This book is richer because of you! To everyone at North Light Books: You all are dream makers in the flesh, talented souls whose creative visions have made this experience a living dream. Thank you. To my collective circle of family and friends who are too many to name, but whose hearts live inside mine. You know who you are. I cannot thank you enough for the endless conversations, the tears, the support, the *a-ha!* moments. I am very clear on the fact that you all have been the whispers of my life, nudging me along to the most honest parts of myself. Thank you.

About the Author

Kelly Rae Roberts grew up in rural northern Florida, where she jumped off docks into the Santa Fe Lake with her German shepherd every day after school. As a child, she lived for eating fried chicken every Sunday afternoon, fishing with an old, tattered piece of bamboo, and playing checkers with her then-eighty-five-year-old granddad. Amidst the winding dirt roads of her hometown, Kelly experienced the joy and complexity of life and, like her mother and sister, turned to creative outlets as a way to express her experiences. Kelly's first memory of her creative gifts being recognized stems from the third grade, when she won a poster contest about dental hygiene that came with a twenty-five-dollar reward, which she promptly used to purchase a Walkman (so she could listen to Michael Jackson and Olivia Newton John—it was 1983, after all!).

In 1985, Kelly's family moved to Jacksonville, where she attended middle and high school. Later, she attended college at Florida State University, majoring in something "practical": social work. In 1999, she met her husband, John, and they set off to begin a life together in Portland, Oregon. There Kelly eventually took up running, which mysteriously led her to discover the confidence and passion to pursue a longtime "impractical" dream: to become an artist.

Kelly has had several articles published in *Cloth Paper Scissors* magazine and has also been featured in many mixed-media books by her peers. Her artwork is collected world-wide, and she is consistently accepted to show at galleries and juried art festivals across the United States. Recently, she entered a variety of long-term licensing agreements that will showcase her work nationwide on cards, journals, magnets, calendars and decorative wall art. Combining her love of art with more than ten years of experience as a clinical social worker, Kelly is skilled at helping others reach for the best parts of themselves, both artistically and personally, in various workshop and art retreat settings, as well in her published articles and musings on her blog.

In essence, Kelly is an artist, social worker and all-around lover of life and people who seeks to express a sense of vitality and connectedness in her creations. Having spent most of her life in the company of women, her pieces grow out of the kindred support she has felt from many of them throughout her life. She is infinitely grateful for the spirits of these women who walk with her, in flesh or in paint, on her incredible journey into art, love and life. Learn more about her at www.KellyRaeRoberts.com, or visit her blog at www.KellyRaeRoberts.blogspot.com.

Contents

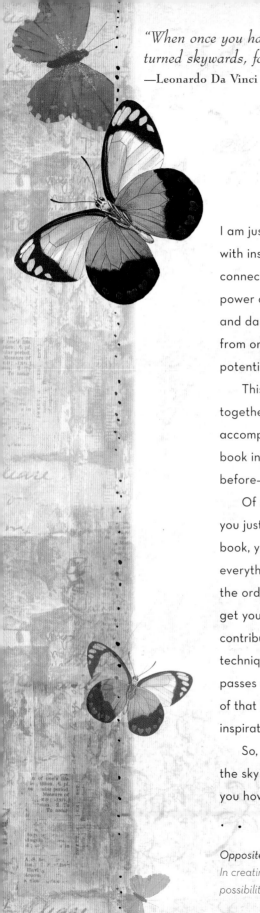

"When once you have tasted flight, you will walk the earth with your eyes turned skywards, for there you have been, and there you will always long to return."
—Leonardo Da Vinci

Introduction

I am just like you. A girl who is always learning. A woman whose soul is vibrant with inspiration. A creative spirit that is expressive and sensitive. We are all connected, intertwining in this creative life. It's because of this that I believe in the power of telling our stories—the stories of how we muster up our courage and leap and dance and breathe our way into our creative dreams. This is how we learn from one another. How we inspire one another. How we begin to finally see the potential and possibilities that live inside our hearts.

This book isn't just my story. It's my conversation with you as we travel together on this journey into our creative spirits. Whether you're a beginner, an accomplished artist or crafter, or somewhere in between, I hope the pages of this book inspire you to see something within yourself that perhaps you didn't notice before—a treasure trove of inspiration found in the depths of your heart.

Of course, taking flight isn't exactly a step-by-step process—sooner or later, you just need to take a deep breath and spread your wings. In the pages of this book, you'll find musings, encouragement, ideas and thoughtful guidance on everything from facing our fears to creating community to finding the sacred in the ordinary. Along the way, thought-provoking prompts and inspiring quotes will get your heart involved in your own creative process. You'll find the work of a few contributing artists, including interviews with these gifted souls. Finally, you'll find techniques—yes, techniques!—in sections titled "Learning to Soar." This book encompasses all aspects of what it means to live the creative life, and an undeniable part of that is learning new methods to incorporate into your own artwork—tangible inspiration you can play with, experiment with, adapt and grow from!

So, come along with me as we find our creative wings and take flight toward the sky of our bliss-filled inspiration—a place where your spirit will soar. I can't tell you how thrilled I am that you are here with me as we explore new paths together!

Opposite page: Winged Promise, 10" × 10" (25cm × 25cm) mixed media on canvas.
In creating this painting, I was inspired by the idea that the promise of flight and creative possibility exists within all of us, that we are born for the journey.

7

Meet Our Inspiring Contributing Artists

My journey into artmaking happened mainly because I was inspired by the spirits and creativity of other artists. Without their ever knowing it, they inspired me to simply begin. To search for my own creative voice. To collage. To paint. To play. So, when I thought about writing this book, I immediately knew I would ask some of my favorite inspirations to contribute. You can only imagine the happy dances inside my heart when they each said yes.

I chose these women because their stories and their art are rich with knowledge, spirit and unique creativity. Some are collage aritsts, painters, sculpturists. And some work in mosaics, assemblage, illustration. Whatever their craft, these are women with heart. With stories. With talent that inspires. Inside the pages of this book, you will find artwork, techniques and interviews with all of them. Think of them as our flight companions as we soar into the sky of our very own creativity.

STEPHANIE LEE

This talented artist writes of her creative journey: "The contours of my heart trace back through history even though my feet have never walked the roads of time other than the short segment I inhabit. A modern day expeditioner, I practice my own version of archaeology, scanning the terrain for intriguing bits and pieces that present themselves—or that are hiding but don't easily escape my grasp. My love of music, words and creative expression (not exclusive to making art) is the morning songbird at my window saying, 'Wake up and get moving! The world won't wait for you to decide you are brilliant. Get up and work anyway!'

"I travel with dear companions who tolerate and encourage my skewed perception of beauty in a world where originality is subjective. I venture out daily with my cockeyed optimism in tow and no particular destination in mind. The only objective being to meet myself somewhere along the path, to grab a friend or two to travel alongside me, to look under what I might otherwise walk right past, to bite into a fresh tomato and feast—letting the juices run down my arms. And always . . . always, always, always, I must indulge in a good laugh whenever possible. To learn more about me, visit www.stephanieleestudios.com and/or www.stephanielee.typepad.com."

MATI ROSE MCDONOUGH

Mati Rose McDonough is thirty-two, but she paints like a sophisticated child. It has taken years for Mati to get to this place of freedom even though she has gone to two schools to study fine art and painting, namely Macalester College and the California College of the Arts. Currently, Mati cuts up doilies to make elephants, silk screens pieces of fennel found by the dumpster, and paints from a place of exploration—all with the impulse to create beauty from the overlooked. Consequently, collage is a natural form of communication for Mati. She has had numerous shows and has published several illustrations, and she hopes this is just the beginning. Along with her talented husband, Hugh D'Andrade, she makes messes and daily discoveries in their shared studio space called Compound 21. You can learn more about her at www.matirose.com.

LAURIE MIKA

Laurie is a mixed-media artist with a passion for combining and overlapping a variety of mediums, creating an original style of mixed-media mosaics and assemblage using handmade tile. Her passion for travel to far-off places and her experiences of living abroad (East Africa) have shaped the way her art looks today, especially since her work is embellished with the many found objects gleaned during her travels. Laurie recently started teaching at national and internationally recognized art retreats such as ArtFest, Art Unraveled, Art and Soul,

and Hacienda Mosaico in Mexico, and next year, she will teach in Tuscany. Combining art with travel is a dream come true for her. Closer to home, Laurie participates in juried shows and has her work in local galleries.

Laurie is the author of *Mixed-Media Mosaics*. Her works have been included in many group shows and galleries, and, in 2007, one of her pieces won Best In Show for 2-D in the Society of American Mosaic Artist exhibition. Her work has also been published in numerous magazines—including *Expression, Somerset Studio, Haute Handbags, Altered Couture, Somerset Studio Gallery* (volume 5), *Somerset Wedding* and *Somerset Home*—and in the books *400 Polymer Clay Designs, Mosaic Art and Style, New Techniques for Wearable Art* and *Beyond Paper Dolls*. Laurie has been featured on HGTV's *Crafters Coast to Coast* and on DIY Network's *Craft Lab*. Learn more about her at www.mikaarts.com.

CHRISTINE MASON MILLER

Christine Mason Miller is a Santa Monica–based artist with more than fifteen years of art, design and illustration experience. She is the creator of the nationally recognized brand Swirly, and her work has been inspiring people of all ages worldwide to make their creative dreams real since 1995. Her work as an artist has since grown and developed far beyond the Swirly world, with collections of paintings and other mixed-media works now being sold and exhibited nationwide. She has filled her portfolio with dozens of works, each of which are part of a different series aimed at capturing experiences large and small that have fueled her creative fire. Christine's very inspiring Web site is www.christinemasonmiller.com.

DJ PETTITT

DJ Pettitt has explored a wide range of craft and fine art interests including wood carving, quilting, oil painting, pastel and colored pencil, and she has received awards for her porcelain paintings. A southern Oregon artist, DJ combines her art background with photography, whimsical face sketches, digital altering and fabric painting, creating mixed-media works in the form of art books, wearable art and giftables. She can be contacted via her Web site, www.djpettitt.com.

JENNIFER VALENTINE

Jennifer Valentine is an assemblage and mixed-media artist who resides in Michigan with her talented husband and five amazing children. Using abandoned and forlorn objects, Jennifer creates a personal line of work that captures the ephemeral nature of those things we cherish and lose through time. Although she's been creating for as long as she can remember, she began her artistic career in 2000 when her artwork was shown at a SoHo gallery. Since then, she has been featured in *Cloth Paper Scissors* magazine, and her artwork has been sold in galleries across the United States. If you'd like to see more of Jennifer's work, please visit her blog at www.sacredcake. blogspot.com or her online marketplace at www.sacredcake. etsy.com. You can email her at sacred_cake@yahoo.com.

JUDY WISE

Judy Wise is an Oregon artist and teacher who has worked as a printmaker and painter for nearly three decades. She believes art connects the hand to the mind to the heart. She can be found online at www.judywise.com or at judywise.blogspot.com.

"What in your life is calling you? When all the noise is silenced, the meetings adjourned, the lists laid aside ... what still pulls on your soul?"
— Terma Collective, "The Box"

CHAPTER ONE

Unearthing Buried Dreams

Do you have an inner voice, a gentle whisper quietly nudging you to listen? What does it say? Does it tell you to begin that creative project you've been putting off? Or does it tell you to dream bigger—perhaps start your own creative business? Maybe it's encouraging you to begin writing that book. Or to travel to exotic places. It may just be a whisper, a small voice tucked deep inside the pockets of your heart, but really, it's your life calling you.

The whispers of our lives want us to take notice, to nurture their message and to discover our own potential. Whether they're quietly nudging us from time to time with long periods of busy silence in between, or annoying us with their persistence, their presence is important and meaningful. We must listen. As Julia Cameron wisely wrote, "We need to listen to the voices within us that want further expression in our lives. We must make the unconscious conscious." This is what it's all about. Acknowledging the voice of our dreams, our creativity, our heart, our lives.

In this chapter, I'll share with you the whispers of my own heart, how I ignored them for most of my life, and how once I started listening to the language of my yearnings, buried dreams became unearthed and creative joy exploded into my life. The same creative joy is possible for you, too, whether you are a stay-at-home mom with a sharp, creative eye or an experienced artist looking for the next step. No matter where we stand in our creative journey, we all have whispers.

I'll also share how listening to the whispers, the callings of our heart, can lead the way to a rediscovery of self, a more creative life and a set of your very own wings. So come along and walk with me, toe-to-toe, on a journey into a creative life. It's a journey wholly possible for you. My hope is that the following pages of this chapter inspire you to listen to your life's callings and give you cause to rediscover your dreams. They are real and possible.

Opposite page: A mixed-media Whispers Art Journal I created from old hardback book covers with the intention to stop and acknowledge my own whispers of heart along the creative journey. Later in this chapter, we'll create another Whispers Art Journal, just for you!

SEARCHING FOR WHISPERS REVEALED

Whispers. We all have them. They're the little voices in our conscious minds that tug at our hearts and want our attention. These whispers, these seeds of dreams, encourage us, even when we're not entirely willing to listen, to simply begin. To begin planning that vacation we've always wanted. To finally start that creative project. To begin writing that book. To write that poem. To work less. To apologize more. They're like little bitty wings, needing the nurturing of our spirits to give them flight into a real and true existence.

Unfortunately, the whispers of our dreams often get suffocated by the constraints and pressures of our everyday lives. If we're not careful, one day leads to another and, before we know it, years have gone by and we've fully neglected them. We don't realize it, but these inner yearnings are our living dreams, our life's possibility today. If we're not conscientious about their presence in our lives, then they get buried underneath the layers of everyday details: cleaning the house, running errands, vacations, house renovations, day jobs. Then, one day, maybe even years later, we wake up and wonder: Who am I, really? What are my passions? What are my dreams for my life and where did they go?

This is exactly what happened in my own life. I did everything I thought I was supposed to do: I went to college and pursued a practical, yet compassionate, career in social work. I went on to get a master's degree and worked for a decade as a medical social worker. In between successful career moves, I fell in love, moved three thousand miles away, got married, bought a house, and settled into a very quiet life of home ownership, a day job, and the occasional vacation. I was so busy building a life, largely on personal and societal expectations, that not once, in all of those years, did I tend to the inner yearnings of a creative life. Not once.

Maybe this hasn't been your experience. Maybe you're a woman who is fully and blissfully in tune with your life's path, a woman whose instincts led the way to a life whole and fulfilling. Perhaps you're right where you want to be, doing exactly what you want to do. And if so, I applaud you. But one thing I've learned along the way is that even the most intuitive and self-aware artist can benefit from testing the limits of her creativity and pushing the boundaries of her comfort zone. Simply getting started down this path can be one of the hardest, most challenging steps of our lives. Perhaps you're not even sure if you have whispers of the heart.

Whispers tend to reveal themselves someplace where they know they'll be safe—like a journal, for instance. If you've ever kept or currently keep a journal, you'll find that reading past, long-forgotten entries can be quite revealing. I've always been a diligent keeper of journals, but you might be surprised to learn that they're not full of art, or even any sketches at all. Peek inside and you'll find pages and pages filled with raw words, pure emotions, my heart spilled out onto graph paper, notebook paper, scrap papers, even napkins. When I look back inside these treasured journals now, I find the voice of a young girl with scribbly handwriting who, at the age of fifteen, was already defining her whispers by writing:

life goals:
become an artist.
learn to paint. to draw.
travel the world.

In fact, even though I did not pursue my art conscientiously until many years after my early journals were written, paging through them now I am surprised to find a telling whisper revealed right there in writing again and again, year after year. Throughout the years of going to college, planning my wedding, interviewing for jobs, I would write:

I feel most balanced when I'm being 'creative', when I'm dreaming of an 'artful' life. I want to expand my creativity and 'learn' how to draw and paint.

So why then did I not listen to those small nudges? Simply put, I suppose I wasn't paying attention in those years. Just as they were written deep in the pages of my old journals, my whispers were tucked deep, deep inside a pocket of my heart for years and years until I would finally begin to listen.

Perhaps your creative journey is already outlined in your journal in black and white—or even in full-color illustrations. Even so, what happens when you read between the lines? Perhaps you are a paper crafter, but time and time again you've written about envying the work of your friends who are painters. Could you have a secret desire to broaden your work, to learn to paint?

Of course, a journal isn't the only place our whispers might show themselves. Have you ever noticed your inner dialogue during quiet moments? I've found that in unexpected quiet places, like when I'm alone in the car or seated on a airplane, my mind wanders and I find myself dreaming of new ideas or plans. Some might call this daydreaming, but it's important to note that our daydreams don't have to be distant, unattainable wishes; they might just be whispers disguised.

How about you? Are your daydreams trying to tell you something? In the spaces between your quiet moments, are your whispers revealed? Perhaps they're in your thoughts just as you drift off to sleep. Or in the soothing moments of taking a bubble bath. All you need to do is learn to listen.

Our whispers also tend to reveal themselves in subtle ways to the people who we feel closest to. They might surface in our letters and e-mails to friends and family. They might even hide beneath the nuances of our everyday conversations. The next time you catch yourself beginning a sentence with, "One day, maybe I can . . ." or, "If I had more time, I would . . ." take notice. Your whispers might be speaking through you in those pure moments of honesty.

If you don't keep a journal, right now is the perfect time to start. We're about to embark on a creative journey together through the pages of this book—one I hope you'll continue on your own. There's no telling what secrets may reveal themselves as we grow and reach and learn together.

LEARNING TO LISTEN

Sometimes we don't pay attention to what is really calling us because we feel limited or even suffocated by decisions we've already made in our lives. We don't give ourselves permission to change, to evolve, to outgrow past decisions. For me, that meant feeling constrained by my decision to choose social work as my major in college, a very practical route. That one decision seemed to pave the way for a sensible, but nonartistic, life for years to come, even though the yearnings of a creative life were all around me. In essence, like so many other young women, I felt stuck inside a decision I had made at a very young age, when I wasn't even sure who I was becoming. Has this ever happened to you? Do you feel strapped down by a decision you made long ago?

Sometimes it's not a past decision that has us feeling stuck, but rather an old role we've historically filled that we can't seem to escape. Perhaps, for you, it was being the task-oriented sibling (while your brother or sister was the "creative one"), the productive partner in your marriage, the practical friend and business partner, the good listener. Could it be that your fulfillment of that role has been preventing you from taking on another? In my case, I was feeling surrounded by creative types— decorators, writers, theater majors, filmmakers, painters—and mistakenly thinking there wasn't room for another creative soul, that the creative role had already been filled.

The good news is that we are so much more than our past decisions and roles. We grow, we change, we evolve. Old decisions and roles may have been very good ones at the time, but we must give ourselves permission to know when it's time to embrace new ones, bit by bit, one step at a time, until we are fully embracing our hearts' whispers, wants and wishes today. If we don't listen to our hearts' callings, we will continue to allow old decisions and comparisons to lead us down uninspiring and grounded paths when, all the while, our creative souls want to take flight.

Our decisions to embrace our whispers come in all sizes. For

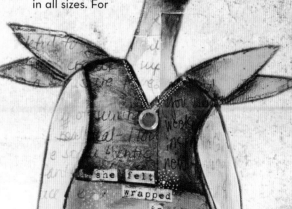

some, they're small commitments to finally carve out a few hours of every weekend for creative messes. For others, they may be a renewed resolve to finally sign up for that knitting class, or perhaps start applying for creative teaching opportunities. And for some, like me, the decision may not seem to have anything to do with living the creative life at all—not at first, anyway.

As I approached my thirtieth birthday, my heart became restless with tangled emotions. I felt ordinary. Passionless. Uncreative. I felt friction in my life, as if my heart knew my life was meant for more joy, but my mind told me everything was fine. After all, I had everything I wanted: a loving marriage, a savings account, my health, a supportive collection of friends and family. I had long forgotten about any creative dreams. They had become deeply buried underneath years of following the practical and safe path. Now, vague yearnings began to resurface, but I was having trouble deciphering what they were trying to tell me.

Like so many young professionals, I had found myself in a place of creative and spiritual unrest. I had successfully laid the groundwork in my early twenties for a career and marriage, but somewhere along the line, I had lost my personal sense of fun, confidence and creativity. For years, my husband, who happened to be very good at following his own bliss, would encourage me to do the same. Like me, he knew I was missing something huge in my life that would bring meaning and joy. But even though I knew I wanted more creativity in my life, I still didn't understand exactly what my whispers were trying tell me. I felt a bit paralyzed, not quite sure what to do, and so, like so many people, I did nothing and went along with my life, all the while knowing deep inside that something was missing—feeling like there must be more.

Do you also struggle with knowing what to do with your whispers? Perhaps today you are feeling something similar to what I experienced years ago. You've listened to your life, you've identified a vague whisper to infuse more creativy into your days, but now you're unsure how and where to begin. Are you doing what I did and questioning your whispers, wondering if there's more to the story? It's an uncomfortable feeling, an instinct that something isn't quite right, but there's an inability to fully describe what it is you may be yearning for. This may mean you're very close, but not quite there. If this is you today, that's OK! Chances are that by reading this book, you're on the right path to deciphering those yearnings. This is where a journal can be very, very helpful. I strongly encourage you, while you read this book, to write down your thoughts. If something pops into your consciousness, write it down. If something calls to you, write it down. Even if something just doesn't quite feel right, jot it down.

Do the same thing as you go through your daily routine. Identify what is speaking to you. Take photos, tear out magazine images, collect quotes and words. Compile it all in a journal of "whisper evidence," and soon you will notice patterns, gentle nudges making themselves known. What are they telling you?

LOOKING WITHIN

By the summer of 2005, my intuition, the whispers of my life, grew louder.

I was jealous of my husband, who seemed to have found his own passion. I wanted to feel that rush of life, too. I wanted the trust of my heart, the energy of life. I wanted the wings. Eventually, when I got quiet with myself, when I peeled away the distractions of my everyday life, when I sat with the questions and longings of my heart, I found a new beginning point. What was my heart telling me all this time in the spaces of waking and dreaming? It was this: Use your hands. Make art. Have more fun. Be less serious. Explore your creativity. But the loudest, most pesky of whispers had nothing to do with living a creative life at all. Instead it was this: Start running.

Start running?

Listening to our whispers doesn't always give us the creative clarity we think it will. I certainly wasn't wishing for a life of running. In fact, I was a bit stunned at this revealed whisper. Running? All that soul-searching, whisper-listening, digging-deeper-stuff to discover an inner voice that said to start running? Really? As our whispers sometimes insist that we do, I went with it. Now, at this point in my life, anyone who knew me knew I wasn't an athlete. I could barely hike three miles without complaints of achy joints and breathlessness. But for me, I needed to do this thing that my whispers were insisting I do. So, when a dear friend encouraged me to join a training program for a half marathon, I signed up with caution, but with an optimism and a renewed sense of joy that beginning something huge gave me. I set out with a goal to run 13.1 miles of one very hilly half marathon.

This is what whispers are all about: challenging your spirit to listen, even if it means doing something you never thought you could do. Especially if it means doing something you never thought you could do. You must do it. The whispers, your instincts, will show you the way. Even if it's not clear at first, you will find your wings.

LIVING WITHOUT LIMITS

Surprisingly, that summer of training for the half marathon changed everything about my life. With each and every training run, I discovered that we learn the most about ourselves when we do the thing we never thought we could do. We unearth our potential. Our limits. Our heart's distance. The whispers get nurtured and our spirits soar.

What is the one thing you never thought you could do? Maybe it has something to do with living the creative life, and maybe it doesn't. That's OK. The point is to pinpoint something, anything that you've always wanted to do but, for some reason or another, never did, perhaps out of fear. Is it something simple, like signing up for a poetry class where you would have to read your poetry aloud? Maybe it's something physical, like biking, or hiking ten miles. Or maybe it's something scarier, like telling the truth about something you've been harboring.

When we actually do the thing we didn't think we could do, something shifts inside of us. We push our boundaries. We find strength in ourselves that we didn't know was there. I have had many friends who have gone through natural childbirth tell me that they got through that experience with a newfound sense of self. That they surprised themselves with their strength, that they, sometimes for the first time in their lives, felt like they could do anything. It's a rush, an adrenaline of spirit. When I started to run, I began to see myself differently. I wasn't a girl who quit early anymore. I wasn't a girl who always said yes. Or a girl who felt limited. Instead, I was a girl who had a voice, a joy, a smile, a very big dream and a purpose. With each crossing of a finish line, my spirit soared with the knowledge that I had finally touched down into the root of my very own possibility. I had conquered something I never thought I would be able to do. Now my world opened up: If I could run, then surely I could paint! The only word I can use to describe what I was feeling in those weeks is limitless.

When we challenge ourselves to push our boundaries, we, perhaps without intending to do so, shed layers of muck—jealousy, perfectionism, worry, fear and self-doubt. Underneath all these shedded layers exists a creative spirit that needs freeing. It's been

there all along, buried beneath misguided intentions. I didn't realize it at the time, but with each run, I was shedding all those very same layers myself. With every finish line (especially the half-marathon finish line!) crossed, I was running, fiercely running back toward myself. The self that was artsy. The self that was fearless. Brave and quirky. Beautifully sensitive. Silly and unique.

My personal journey through doing the one thing I didn't think I could do taught me the invaluable, life-changing lesson that anything is possible in our lives when we stop denying ourselves the chance to see our own potential. With that huge lesson learned and tucked into the pockets of my heart, I felt free to explore my creative wings— the real whispers of my heart. The ones that suggested I begin painting. To simply begin. To create a space and time to play with paper and paint. To embrace the rawness of a starting point. This is when the world of artful living finally entered my life. It's a small but significant miracle in my life, to have recognized and embraced this awakening.

The same is possible for you. Listen to your whispers. Identify them. Follow their truth. Hold possibility close to your chest and allow it to step into the light and give your creative spirit a chance. Do the thing that scares you the most. By doing it, you'll give birth to your life's promise and unearth your buried dreams. Rediscover your worth, your potential, your creative spirit. Then go and fly on its wings to places you won't ever want to leave.

Three mixed-media spreads from my *Whispers Art Journal*, all painted on old hardback book covers.

From left to right: Flying on the Wings of Dreams, She Learned to Cup Possibility in her Hands *and* Some Dreams of Mine. *Creating these pages encouraged me to acknowledge my creative calling and to understand that there lies great possibility in our lives when we hold on tight to it and let it show us the way.*

she learned
to cup possibility
in her hands

some [small + big]
dreams
of
mine...

open a shoppe with my mom
make really big art
roam europe in flip-flops
sleep under the moon
cherish the small moments
have a solo show
write love poems

In the depths of my heart, creative dreams are calling me to take notice. They are:

The one thing I never thought I could do is:

Here's how I can make a plan to do it:

Who in my life has passion? What questions could I ask her/him about her/his story?

I feel most inspired when:

"Inside you there's an artist you don't know about . . . Say yes quickly, if you know, if you've known it from before the beginning of the universe." —RUMI

"Children, like animals, use all their senses to discover the world. Then artists come along and discover it the same way, all over again." —EUDORA WELTY

"If you hear a voice within you say 'you cannot paint,' then by all means paint, and that voice will be silenced." —VINCENT VAN GOGH

"If you keep doing what you've always done, you'll keep getting what you've always gotten." —ANONYMOUS

"The deepest secret is that life is not a process of discovery, but a process of creation. You are not discovering yourself, but creating yourself anew. Seek, therefore, not to find out Who You Are, seek to determine Who You Want to Be." —NEALE DONALD WALSCH

"When nothing is sure, everything is possible." —MARGARET DRABBLE

"The openness to begin is all the openness required to have each day. We start today, and tomorrow we start again, and the day after we start again, as we will the day after that. In this way does our journey come to us. We begin. The rest unfolds through us." —JULIA CAMERON

Taking Flight with
CONTRIBUTING ARTIST DJ Pettitt

KRR: DJ, you have been such an inspiration to me and countless others who embrace the creative path. Can you share with us a little bit about your own flight into artmaking?

DJ: For as long as I can remember, I wanted to be an artist. Many in my family are/were creative in different ways, from quilting to woodworking, so I had a lot of exposure and experience using my hands creatively while growing up. We ate what we grew, wore handmade clothing and slept under handmade quilts, so it was very natural for me to continue in that path.

KRR: Growing up in a creative environment, did you still have personal whispers and inner yearnings to embrace a creative life? If yes, how did you nurture that calling? What were the challenges?

DJ: While in high school, I dreamt of attending art school and eventually teaching art at a high-school level. Art classes were lacking in my school, and the extent of art education was limited at best. My biggest challenge preventing those dreams from coming to fruition was having to quit college. The yearnings never left me, though, and stayed throughout the trials of growing up and many life changes.

Several years later, I had the opportunity to take some local oil painting classes, and I haven't stopped learning and growing in my art since. In the past twenty-five years, I have tried many different types of art media, and through it all, I always knew that one day I would find my niche. Little did I know that thirty years after those dreams of teaching art, I would return to that first love and be teaching art at workshops around the country.

KRR: I think it's interesting and wonderful that you always had longings to teach and here you are now. You've unearthed an early dream of your own! As a teacher, what is it like to witness your students listening to their own whispers by signing up for your art class? For many of them, I'm sure it's something they've never done before.

DJ: You have hit on one of the most rewarding parts of teaching. I love meeting students who have never picked up a brush, or who have painted very little before coming to class, and they leave giddy with excitement as they realize they can paint! It's so fun to watch them go from overwhelmed, as they enter class, to smiling and confident as they leave. Also, the connection that I have with students one on one during class time is very fulfilling. Everyone signs up for a different reason and with different goals and expectations. It is a joy to try and meet them where they are in their art and to focus on their whispers as I watch them take flight.

KRR: I love that you do, indeed, meet your students where they are. Some of them are teachers themselves. Some have never picked up a paintbrush. I've seen the artwork that comes out of your classes, and have been blown away by it. Do you think that we always have these little whispers, no matter where we are in our process? Or are they just stronger the longer they've been neglected?

DJ: Yes, both! I think that the whispers are always there—and that they get stronger the longer they are neglected. For as long as I can remember, I have had a need to create. I haven't always known what I needed to create, or how, but I have always felt it and known that it was there. As I nurture and listen to those longings, my art continually changes and grows, along with the endlessly changing whispers.

Opposite page: Listening to the Whispers, *mixed-media, one-of-a-kind tote by contributing artist extraordinaire DJ Pettitt. DJ is an expert at painting endearing and whimsical figures on fabric. She often turns these fabric paintings into gorgeous, one-of-a-kind, hand-sewn totes like this one.*

Learning to Soar

In this section, we get to play! Let's get our hands blissfully dirty in paint, glue and other supplies while we make an art journal out of old hardback book covers. Perhaps this journal can be a place where you can jot down your whispers as they reveal themselves to you. Whatever you decide to do with your journal, I'm sure you will love the process of making it.

For this project, and for all of the "Learning to Soar" projects throughout this book, I've combined some of my own techniques along with this chapter's contributing artist's techniques into one work. Learning how to incorporate the contributor techniques into these pieces allowed me to stretch outside my comfort zone and learn new things. It also provided an opportunity to take their methods and make them my own—just as I am encouraging you to do with everything you learn in this book. So come along with me as we both learn something new!

First we'll learn DJ's technique for painting on fabric. Then I'll share some of my own processes for creating painted collages on hardback book covers. Finally, we'll combine the two as we assemble our very own Whispers Art Journal.

MATERIALS FOR PAINTING ON FABRIC

strip of 1" × 4" (3cm × 10cm) cotton-blend patterned fabric

scraps of other patterned fabrics

fusible interfacing

fluid acrylics

foam brush

stiff fabric brush

hard pencil

clear gesso

Heat 'n Bond, iron-on adhesive

iron

ironing board

damp press cloth

scissors

brayer (optional)

paper towel (optional)

MATERIALS FOR CREATING A WHISPERS ART JOURNAL

2 hardback books	Stabilo black pencil
patterned papers	graphite pencil
varying random lengths of ribbon	white gel pen
Shiva Artist's Paintstiks in assorted colors	gel medium
fluid acrylics	brayer
palette paper	eyelet setter
paintbrush	razor
fine detail paintbrush	hammer
black fine-point Faber-Castell PITT Artist Pen	damp paper towel

PAINTING ON FABRIC {Contributing Artist's Technique by DJ Pettitt}

For this part of the project, we're going to use DJ's technique to create fabric A-R-T letters that will hang from the journal's binding. In making DJ's technique my own, I decided to use her method of preparing fabric, then "piecing" it together to create texture and a patchwork of color. I then painted over it in my own style. Working with fabric was new for me, and I learned so much, including the benefits of fabric paintbrushes and clear gesso (which I didn't even know existed!).

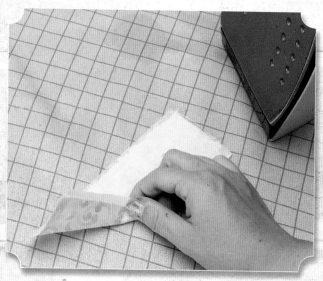

Step 1 ... CUT FABRIC AND IRON ON INTERFACING

Use scissors to cut a strip of patterned fabric to about 1" × 4" (3cm × 10cm). Rip the edges to create a subtle frayed look. Place the coated side of the interfacing on the wrong side of the fabric. Cover it with a damp press cloth, and iron the fabric on medium steam according to the manufacturer's instructions for the interfacing.

Step 2 ... BUILD AND BOND FABRIC COLLAGE

Cut out small pieces of coordinating patterned fabrics in any shapes you like. Arrange them in a fabric collage over the surface of your strip. Use Heat 'n Bond to adhere all of the small pieces onto the strip, following the manufacturer's instructions.

Step 3 ... DRAW ON FABRIC AND COAT WITH GESSO

Use a hard pencil to draw the letters "A" "R" "T" (or spell the word of your choice) over the surface of the fabric collage. Add some doodles or sketches if you'd like. Use a foam brush to coat the fabric with a layer of clear gesso, and let it dry completely. The gesso will seal the fabric and provide surface tooth for painting.

Stretch Your Wings

Explore other ways to paint on fabric. For example, DJ often transfers copies of her sketches onto fabric using gel medium and then paints the transfers. In any case, it's important to coat your fabric with clear gesso first to help eliminate unwanted pattern lines and prepare your surface for any type of paint.

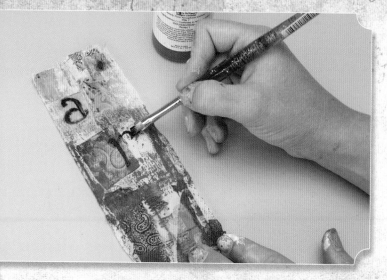

Step 4 ... PAINT FABRIC COLLAGE AND CUT INTO PIECES

Mix some fluid acrylic paints and use a brayer, a brush or a paper towel to apply it randomly to your fabric collage surface. (For this piece I used a brayer to add shades of pink and brown.) With a fabric brush, use fluid acrylic paints to paint your letters. With scissors, cut the strip into three squares, one letter serving as the focal point of each piece.

CREATING A WHISPERS ART JOURNAL

Now I'll share my techniques on how to create the art journal itself using old hardback book covers. You'll also learn how to create a patchwork collage painting using patterned papers and my favorite tool in my studio: the brayer! This project also cross-references a couple of techniques outlined, step-by-step, elsewhere in the book. (It's always fun to see a technique in action in more ways than one!) In the end, it will all come together into one journal of whispers.

Step 5 ... REMOVE COVERS FROM HARDBACK BOOKS

Use a razor to cut the front and back covers off of 2 hardback books.

Stretch Your Wings

Try using the covers of different types of hardback books. I really like to use square hardback book covers, and sometimes really large ones, too.

Step 6 ... CREATE COVER COLLAGE

Begin decorating the front cover with a collage of patterned paper. Adhere the pieces with gel medium until you've established a composition. Brush gel medium over the surface. Let it dry. Using the oil painting technique shown on pages 105–107, paint a face in a corner of your work. This needs to dry for 24 hours before you can add details to the face with other art mediums. In the meantime, load your brayer with liquid acrylic paint (I used orange and pink) and randomly roll the color over the paper collage, being careful to avoid the face area of your subject. While the paint is still wet, use a damp paper towel to rub off areas of paint to reveal the papers in the background.

Step 7 ... DRAW AND PAINT SUBJECT AND HAMMER HOLES

With a Stabilo black pencil, draw in the outline of your subject. Color her in with some fluid acrylic paint and wipe it away with a paper towel to reveal parts of the paper collage that you want to show through. (Here I used two shades of pink for my subject's dress.) Using an eyelet setter (I like the bigger ones), hammer 2 holes ⅛" (3mm) from the edge and 1" (3cm) from the top and from the bottom. These will enable you to bind the book later. Using your graphite pencil, give your subject wings and smudge the lines with your finger for a softer look. Use your white gel pen to add other details (here I drew a collar and a belt).

Step 8 ... CREATE INTERIOR PAGES AND PUNCH HOLES

Paint or collage the other 3 book covers from step 1 however you'd like. These will serve as the interior pages of your journal. (I created colorful but not overpowering backgrounds upon which I could later write my thoughts.) Line them up under the front cover and use a pencil or pen to trace the holes you punched in step 7. Use the hammer and the eyelet setter to then punch 2 holes in each of these pieces, as well. Punch a hole in the top center of each of the 3 pieces of fabric. Gather all of the components for the book together to prepare to bind them.

Step 9 ... ASSEMBLE JOURNAL

Align all of your pages so the holes line up. Select some pieces of ribbon at varying lengths, and string the pages together in each hole, tying them however you choose. Be sure to include an extra-long ribbon in the top hole, and thread the cloth "A" "R" "T" pieces through this ribbon so that they land at different lengths.

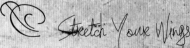 *Stretch Your Wings*

Be sure to paint the backgrounds on your interior pages before hammering the holes; otherwise the holes can be clogged with paint.

Step 10 ... FINISH FACE ON JOURNAL COVER

Once your oil paint from step 6 has dried completely, add details to the facial features with a white gel pen, fine-point Faber-Castell PITT Artist Pen, fluid acrylics and a Stabilo black pencil as detailed on page 107.

Step 11 ... WRITE ON INSIDE PAGES

Now you're ready to journal your thoughts on the pages inside the book. I used a black pen to ensure my letters would be legible against the bold background.

Stretch Your Wings

Try adding other embellishments to your journal—perhaps adding some beading to your ribbon or a favorite quote on the cover. The possibilities are endless!

"What I emphasize is for people to make choices based not on fear, but on what really gives them a sense of fulfillment."
—Pauline Rose Chance

CHAPTER TWO

Facing Your Fears

Sometimes our fears get the best of our creative potential. Sometimes we go far too long making one decision after the next from a place of fear. We choose what feels comfortable and easy, what brings more money or the least amount of change and, often, what would give us a sense of control. Then, when we finally listen to our whispers, we have different fears. These fears, with their persuading voices, try to sabotage our creative dreams.

For me, my creative fears sound like this: Who do I think I am? What if my work isn't good enough? What if I'm not talented enough? What if I can't make a living doing something I love? Perhaps yours are different, but they're still there, discouraging you every step of the way. Quite often, our fears are the perfect counterpart to our whispers. Our whispers say, "Go for it. You are enough." But our fears fire back with, "You're not strong enough," or "You'll never be as talented as so-and-so." But if we learn not only to trust but also to own our talent, our wishes, our dreams, then we can make decisions not from a place of fear, but rather from a place of deep-rooted hope and faith. This may seem unnatural at first, this idea of going against all the fears we've collected in our lives, but doing it will take you to a more meaningful existence that feels refreshingly more like yourself.

In this chapter, I'll share with you my own struggles and fears that arose as I began to embrace the creative life. I'll share how I recognize them, how I manage them from where I stand today and how I'm learning to embrace them. They do, after all, have something to show and teach us. Sometimes, we just need to sit with them for a while, face their direction, take notice, then take action.

My hope is that the following pages will inspire you to identify your fears and then, little by little, release them as you take small steps toward whatever creative dreams are calling your spirit. May you remember your eight-year-old self—the self that was brave and wildly perfect and creative. And may that spirit, your spirit, give you permission to step outside the shadow of your fears.

Opposite page: Fearless Wings Just for Her, 8" × 8" (20cm × 20cm) mixed-media patchwork collage painting on canvas. I painted this piece as a reminder to be bold, brave and fearless on the creative path. I'll share with you my patchwork collage techniques on pages 104-105.

29

CONFRONTING YOUR SUBCONSCIOUS

Fears are pesky and persuasive little buggers. If we're not careful, they help themselves to the creative landscape of our hearts, planting roots and spreading their tangled web of weeds all over our creative dreams. Tangled in the web are fears of failing, of losing money, of not being inspired, and so on. Sometimes that web gets so dense that it's hard for our creative spirit to breathe, to dream new dreams or to simply begin.

Unknowingly, we give our fears, that web of weeds, more energy and landscape to grow upon every time we delay our creative longings. We convince ourselves that we'll get started on that creative project "after we get married," or "after things settle down a bit," or "after the kids start school." I don't know about you, but it took me years to recognize this harmful pattern in my life. When we delay our creative yearnings, we, in essence, live in a world of procrastinating our creative truth because we are afraid of it. We, maybe without even knowing it, continue to allow our fears and doubts to swallow our creative spirit. Perhaps this where you are today, waiting, waiting, waiting for that perfect time that will never arrive. It's always hanging out there, like an elusive dangling reward that you can't ever seem to reach. Eventually, we give up because that perfect time never arrives. And the hard truth is that it may never arrive. We'll never have enough money, enough time, enough support. And all of us, yes all of us, will always have fears trying to keep our creative unfolding at bay.

But here's the liberating and gentle truth: Your creative spirit is very, very forgiving. It doesn't care where you're going, or how busy you are, or if the house is clean, or even if you're afraid. It just wants you to recognize it from where you stand today—even with the hectic schedule, the overwhelming moments, the worries, and the ever-growing to-do list. We must embrace the idea that our creative dreams can begin from the very place we stand today, not "after this" or "after that" or when everything else in our lives lines up perfectly.

I wrestled with my own fears (and still do) before I embraced the creative life. I worried that I had missed my opportunity and that I wouldn't be able to make a successful career move from practical social worker to artist. I had fears about whether or not my work would be accepted or if I had any natural talent. But one thing became clear to me as I wrestled with my doubts and worries: I must make a clear decision, a commitment to my creative wishes in order to see any potential progress. Just as with love when we make a decision about the kind of person we want to be with, I had to make a very clear decision about the kind of life I really wanted before I took real flight into my creativity.

Wherever you are in your path, your creative bliss wants you to choose its spirit and give it a chance, to let its wisdom shine in your life. It's likely been standing in the shadows of all those practical fears, patiently waiting for you to notice, to allow it to step into the light. Sometimes making this choice can be daunting, a struggle between the heart and the mind.

In the months before making my own decision, my husband and I moved to California. An Oregonian at heart, I wasn't thrilled to leave our home in Portland, but I took the move as an opportunity to embrace the idea of switching gears. I daydreamed about forgoing a full-time social work position and instead getting a part-time job so I could focus on my art and perhaps sell it as a way to supplement our expenses in California. I thought to myself, why not? What's the worst that can happen? This is when the real fears kicked in.

I could fail. I could fall flat on my spirit and fail. I could give up a guaranteed income of a day job and risk everything. What if nobody bought anything? What if I wasn't good enough? Who did I think I was? I had just started painting a few months ago. I wasn't ready. Could I handle the rejection? What would my family think? Shouldn't I be more responsible and, in fact, take a step in the opposite direction, maybe even get two full-time jobs to help pay for my husband's tuition instead of being unrealistic about my lofty artistic dreams?

Perhaps all of this sounds familiar—the endless sea of questions and fears that try and sabotage our creative whispers. Sometimes we just have to sit with it all while we try to move forward with our dreams in spite of our fears.

What small step can you take today? Could you perhaps create a small, welcoming space in your home where you can spread out your collage materials, your scrapbooking papers, your photographs? Remember, our creativity isn't asking for a bold leap into uncertainty—often our largest fear of all, the one that keeps us from beginning. It just wants us to take action in spite of our fears, just a small step from where we are today, nothing too intimidating.

Perhaps you're not quite sure what's stopping you from taking a small step or two toward your creativity or new creative direction. This is a great time to get out your journal, your pens and brushes, your heart. Instead of staying clear of your fears, face them. Sit with them awhile. Ask them questions. And ask yourself what you're afraid of, what's holding you back. Write it all down in your journal. Once you're able to identify your fears, you have a much better chance of diffusing them. If you're like me, you'll find they don't seem nearly as intimidating or vague once you're able to give them a name and identity.

Then, while you still have your journal in front of you, make a list of affirmations, or direct responses to each of your fears. For example, if your fear says, "You aren't good enough," you might write, "You are enough." If your inner critic says, "You're not brave enough," you might write, "Leap fearlessly!" Soon, you'll have your own list of personal declarations from your heart to help battle your fears. This technique, by the way, is how I came up with my own personal affirmations for the artwork on page 33 called *Let It Go*.

TAKING A (BIG) SMALL STEP
Just weeks before we moved, I was visiting my best friend Gina in the mountains of North Carolina and I wrote this in my journal:

The clarity I've had up here nestled in the mountains, in between naps in my favorite hammock, is that I need to do art. I need it. I need to pursue it, in earnest, in Oakland, California. I need to get a social work job, but only part-time (we do need to eat, after all) and I need to give this life, this art in my heart, in my mind, in my thoughts, a real chance to breathe and dance and live. And we'll see where that leap will take me. This is my promise to myself. This is my chance. Those fears of how we'll make it, where the money will come from, will have to find another pocket in some other heart. Mine is clear now.

For me, it came down to identifying, then embracing, my fears about the life I was envisioning, and making a decision, a choice to fly or to stay still. I wanted to fly. I was caught by inspiration. It had a firm grip on my soul, and it was leading the way. I just needed to pay attention and take action.

How about you? Where are you today, in spirit? Are you ready to make your decision? Of course, it may not be the same as mine. Perhaps you're not looking to enter the world of selling your work at all. Perhaps your decision is one that involves getting started on that idea you've had tucked away for awhile. Or perhaps it's learning a new craft you've always wanted to try. Whatever the case, the first small step is making the decision, one heartfelt, committed "yes" to your creative thoughts and dreams. Then the next step is to take action, one small step after another.

By the way, I hear a lot of people talk about "taking the leap" as if they're jumping off some tall platform into a huge deep puddle of uncertainty. Instead, reframe it for yourself. Focus on doable, attainable steps. And when you do think of taking that leap, instead of visulaizing a leap downward, think of a leap upward, toward the sky of your potential. When we take small steps to provide a little nourishment to our creative wings, we leap and bound toward a creative joy so huge we wonder why we didn't do it long ago. The fears disappear. Our courage expands. Our dreams become more and more a part of our daily existence. We take flight into a life less fearful, more free, more creative.

For me, action means a number of things. It means giving my life a voice and my fears and inner critic something to think about. It means putting artwork up for sale just to see what happens. It means submitting applications to juried art festivals with a hopeful heart, even if I have no idea what I'm doing. It means buying a fancy printer and scanner and offering prints. It means learning how to make a Web site. It means attending art retreats alone, ready to learn. It means embracing community. It means submitting articles and works to my favorite magazine just to see if they call back. It means one step at at time. One fear at a time. One day at a time.

What does taking action look like for you? Perhaps you are an illustrator wanting to license your work. Perhaps your small step is researching licensing options. Perhaps you're a scrapbooking artist looking to share your work with the world. Why not put together a portfolio and send it off to your favorite design teams? Actions come in all sizes. Soon you'll be leaping your way from one small step to the next until you find yourself right where you want to be: in the middle of a life you've always wanted. By taking action, you attract to your life the same mindful intention you put into it.

REMEMBERING HOW TO BE FEARLESS

Taking action against fear also means embracing the notion of unlearning ourselves—breaking down the walls we've built to keep us safe until we see ourselves as we did when we were eight years old: brave, creative, curious, alive. So often, we think the older we get, the more answers we'll have. We associate wisdom with age. While there's some truth to this, perhaps we can, in realilty, best associate our true, uninhibited selves with who we were when we were younger. I think we knew who we were, in essence and in pure creative spirit, when we were eight, nine, ten years old, before we let fear enter our world and spoil our vision. Who were you in those years? What did you love to do? What made you happy? What would your life be like if you reclaimed that spirit, that childlike wonder, and made it part of who you are today?

For me, remembering my younger self was a lot like becoming a runner, when my thinking began to shift from a place of fear and into a place of limitlessness. I believe this is possible for all of us. We can begin to see and remember the best parts of ourselves, and in turn, begin to surrender ourselves to our very own possibility. We can remember our fearless selves, our inspired selves, our joyful selves. It's all possible. One step at a time. We were born for this journey—fears, struggles, love, inspiration, all of it. And we were born with a set of our very own wings. Sometimes, we just have to rediscover them.

Of course, we can't expect our fears to disappear overnight. Often, just when we think they've left us, we find they've cleverly transformed themselves instead. In my journey, this is evident in a journal entry I wrote as things were starting to unfold in my creative life and I was beginning to enjoy some success:

In my moodiness and quietness the last few days, I've had some weird feelings of fear, fear of being "found out." It's a strange and vague sense that I've fooled everyone into thinking that I'm thoughtful, talented and worthy of success, when on the inside it feels more like inadequacy. My film-maker friend Kat calls it the "impostor syndrome"—when you're worried that others are realizing that you're not so talented or smart after all, and that you just fooled them all into thinking so.

In hindsight, I was fearing my own potential, my own light, my own talents! What a change—I had journeyed through the whispers, through the fears of beginning, through the tangled web of finally settling into a creative life, and now I was fearing my own success and joy! I was right back where I had started: Who did I think I was? Only this time, it was, Who did I think I was to be having so much fun and enjoying life so much?

Has this happened to you? Do you think you're having too much fun sewing those adorable sock monsters or scrapbooking your memories or painting to your heart's delight? Try not to doubt this blissful feeling. It's your creative spirit soaring. This is what it's supposed to feel like! We must, above all else, own our joy, and our journey into our creativity. We've earned this feeling of soaring. After all, we've faced the very direction of our fears, identified them, made a choice to take small steps in spite of them, and now here we are taking flight into our creative dreams. This is what we were meant to do. Don't forget to celebrate!

Let It Go, 6" × 12" (15cm × 30cm) mixed media on canvas. This painting was a direct response to my inner fears. If my fears said, "You can't do it," then I responded with, "Surrender your fear." If my inner critic bounced back with, "You don't know what you're doing," I responded more forcefully: "Unleash your intuition!" Before long, I had a whole list of personal affirmations to use in this painting—a very powerful piece that gave my creative voice strength and determination. I encourage you to make your own list to combat any fears you may be facing today.

Winged Thoughts

The last time I felt free-spirited, courageous and uninhibited in my creativity, I was:

When it comes to my creativity, these are the fears I most need to recognize so I can move past them:

If I wasn't afraid, I would:

When it comes to embracing my creative hopes today, I can start with these small steps:

"Our deepest fear is not that we are inadequate. Our deepest fear is that we are powerful beyond measure. It is our light, not our darkness that most frightens us. We ask ourselves, 'Who am I to be brilliant, gorgeous, talented, fabulous?' Actually, who are you not to be? . . . And as we let our light shine, we unconsciously give other people permission to do the same." —MARIANNE WILLIAMSON

"Faith is the daring of the soul to go farther than it can see." —WILLIAM NEWTON CLARK

"When you follow your bliss . . . doors will open where you would not have thought there would be doors, and where there wouldn't be a door for anyone else." —JOSEPH CAMPBELL

"Learn to unlearn." —BENJAMIN DISREALI

"Twenty years from now you will be more disappointed by the things you didn't do than by the ones you did do." —MARK TWAIN

" . . . The moment one definitely commits oneself, then providence moves too. All sorts of things occur to help one that would never otherwise have occurred." —JOHANN WOLFGANG VON GOETHE

"I believe that courage is all too often mistakenly seen as the absence of fear. If you descend by rope from a cliff and are not fearful to some degree, you are either crazy or unaware. Courage is seeing your fear, in a realistic perspective, defining it, considering alternatives and choosing to function in spite of risks." —LEONARD ZUNIN

"The death of fear is in doing what you fear to do." —SEQUICHIE COMINGDEER

"You can't be afraid of stepping on toes if you want to go dancing." —LEWIS FREEDMAN

"Fear is the reason for making art. It is a means to freedom." —ILYA KABAKOV

"Without fear and illness, I could never have accomplished all I have." —EDVARD MUNCH

"Do one thing every day that frightens you." —ELEANOR ROOSEVELT

Taking Flight with
CONTRIBUTING ARTIST Laurie Mika

KRR: You are a woman who, to me, seems fearless. Do you remember a time when you had fears about living the creative life? What sort of fears are you facing today?

LM: My desire to create has always been a natural part of my persona. I would live the creative life even if I never sold or exhibited my art. However, the decision to put one's work out there is where facing one's fears comes into play. The biggest fear was, of course, rejection, that people wouldn't like what I did, that they wouldn't connect with my art and that they certainly wouldn't buy it! The way I overcame this fear was to do exactly that: Put it out there. It is like exposing oneself and thereby making oneself truly vulnerable. It takes courage to overcome fear, but it is the process of summoning this courage in the deep recesses of one's psyche that enables us to battle with the demons of insecurity. The confidence gained by winning a battle or two helps to make conquering fear that much easier the next time around.

Each step in living the creative life is often filled with trepidation. I can't tell you the anxiety I felt when I decided to teach for the first time! Self-doubt surfaced, and I panicked at the thought of what I was facing. However, I realized that confronting those fears was the only way to overcome them, so I accepted the challenge.

Since then, the things I was fearful about have changed. These days, trying to juggle everything and manage my time is a constant source of stress. My fear is that when I feel so overwhelmed with the demands of keeping the success going, my creative voice will abandon me and the wellspring of ideas will dry up! Based on past experience, I know this, too, will pass.

KRR: Can you describe that feeling when you realize you really can go farther than you had ever dreamed?

LM: I seem to have that feeling more and more these days! The experiences that I have had in the past four years since I started teaching have been amazing. I've found that the more I challenge myself and overcome the fears and obstacles that once held me back, the more willing I am to do things I would never have considered a few years ago. Students in my workshops often ask if I worry about sharing the techniques I have developed over the last eighteen years. My answer is that I have gained so much more by putting it out there. If I had succumbed to early fears about people copying what I did, then I would have hoarded what I knew, and I would still be in my small world, by myself. The world has become BIG because sharing knowledge is a way to connect with people everywhere. What goes around comes around, and the good that one does comes back tenfold. Facing my fears has given me the confidence to live the life I imagined!

KRR: Do you have any advice for women who are beginning down their creative paths who may be juggling their own worries while nurturing their creative visions?

LM: I am so amazed by the number of young women who have already found their creative voices. My humble advice would be to try to find balance by setting aside time to create and making it a priority in one's life. It is so easy to get distracted by the minutiae of daily living! I often feel guilty about letting things slide around the house, but I have come to realize that I can't do it all. I can't be a great cook, a great housekeeper, and a great gardener and still keep my art a priority in my life. Some people might be able to do that but not me. Through the child-rearing years, my art took a back seat until [my kids] were all in school. I wanted to enjoy my kids and spend those precious years together. It would have been pure frustration if I had tried to juggle too many things when they were young. My only other small morsel of advice would be to accept one's limitations and embrace those things that are the most important in your life.

Opposite page: Worry Doll *mixed-media mosaic by our talented contributing artist Laurie Mika. Inspired by the traditional Guatemalan worry dolls, Laurie nailed her actual fears into this expressive and sincere piece.*

Learning to Soar

It's that time again: We get to make a happy mess while we create a new project. Remember, we're in this together—don't be afraid to try something new!

First, we'll learn Laurie's brilliant techniques for using polymer clay, paints and embellishments. Wait, you've never worked with polymer clay before? That's OK—it was new to me, too, and I confess I was totally intimidated! I wasn't sure if I could make it my own, but after jumping in, I loved it—and I can honestly say I will surely use it again. We'll be creating a clever dimensional dress form, and while it bakes, we'll make a painted collage, keeping in mind that we'll later feature the finished clay form as a focal point. I'll share some of my favorite ways to use ordinary household objects to apply paint in a way that creates a texture-rich and interesting background. In the end, we'll have combined a little bit of Laurie's style with my own for one finished piece. In the process, my initial fear quickly turned into an opportunity to reach and stretch and play, and I have faith that yours will too.

MATERIALS FOR CREATING A POLYMER CLAY DRESS FORM

3 packages of Pearl Premo! polymer clay

polymer stamps (Character Constructions)

"Wishes" metal art embellishment (K&Company)

rhinestone bezels

fluid acrylics in Burnt Umber and other various colors

Walnut Stain Distress Ink (Ranger)

gold mica dust

paintbrush

piece of ceramic tile (or another heat-safe work surface that can be baked with the clay)

toaster oven or conventional oven

rolling pin

paper towels

MATERIALS FOR ADDING TEXTURE WITH HOUSEHOLD ITEMS

7" × 7" (18cm × 18cm) block of wood

gesso

Naples Yellow Hue, Titan Buff, brown, red, blue, white and black fluid acrylic paints

palette paper

paintbrush

charcoal pencil

extra-heavy gel medium

small, round plastic lid

textured, nonstick shelf liner

bubble wrap

spray bottle of water

paper towels

CREATING A POLYMER CLAY DRESS FORM
{ Contributing Artist's Technique by Laurie Mika }

As you can see from Laurie's gorgeous piece on page 36, she is quite the expert at creating beautiful mosaic tiles from polymer clay. In an effort to make her technique feel more like "me," I decided to create a dress form that would fit with my own style of art. This turned out to be a great way to get inspired and learn something new without stepping completely outside my comfort zone and attempting a mosaic piece.

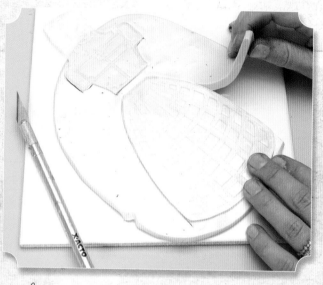

Step 1 ... CONDITION, STAMP AND CUT POLYMER CLAY

Condition and roll out 3 packages of Pearl-colored Premo! polymer clay on a piece of ceramic tile to about ¼" (6mm) thickness using a rolling pin. Lay the polymer stamps from Character Constructions over the clay and press them firmly into the clay to impress the images of the skirt and torso. Leaving the stamps in place for ease of cutting, use a craft knife to cut around the images. Then remove the stamps.

Step 2 ... PAINT CLAY DRESS FORM

Brush acrylic paint over the clay, smudging it from time to time with a damp paper towel to get a faded look. Here I used Burnt Umber Light fluid acrylic paint. Select or mix a complementary color of paint and use a paper towel to rub it over some areas to give them more depth and variation of color.

Step 3 ... ADD DEPTH OF COLOR WITH ACCENT INK

Rub the Walnut Stain Distress Ink pad directly over the painted surface to pick up the stamped texture of the skirt.

Step 4 ... ADD SPARKLE WITH GOLD MICA DUST

Sprinkle some gold mica dust lightly over the surface.

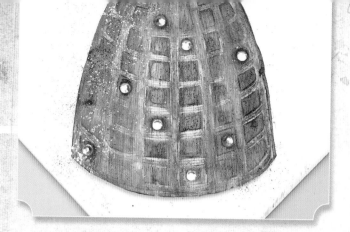

Step 5 ... ADD DECORATIVE EMBELLISHMENTS

Press some rhinestone bezel embellishments firmly into the clay.

Step 6 ... PAINT AND EMBELLISH TOP PIECE OF DRESS FORM

Paint the top portion of the clay in a color that matches the skirt, rub the Walnut Stain Distress Ink pad over the painted surface, sprinkle it with some gold mica dust, and add a metal art embellishment. Bake the clay on the ceramic tile in an oven according to the manufacturer's instructions. Set it aside.

ADDING TEXTURE WITH HOUSEHOLD ITEMS

While our dress form bakes, we'll prepare a richly textured background by transforming household items into tools for applying paint. I'll show you my secrets here before adding the form created with Laurie's techniques to create one finished work. This is a very fun and messy way to paint, so put on your aprons and let's go!

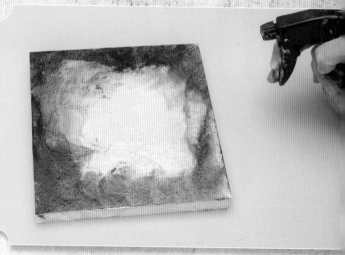

Step 7 ... GESSO, PAINT AND BLEND BACKGROUND

Brush a coat of gesso onto your block of wood and let it dry. To begin your painted background, brush some Naples Yellow Hue onto the surface and allow it to dry. Drip some Titan Buff onto the first layer of yellow paint and rub it in with a paper towel to create a muted hue around the borders.

Step 8 ... LAYER PAINT AND SPRAY WATER

Mix some brown and red fluid acrylic paints and rub them around the outer rim of the surface with a paper towel. Spray some water onto the wet paint.

41

Step 9 ... BLOT SURFACE

Let the water sit for a few minutes and then blot it off with a paper towel.

Step 10 ... TRANSFER TEXTURED PATTERN TO SURFACE

Brush paint randomly onto a piece of textured, nonstick shelf liner. Press it down onto your painted background to transfer a bit of the pattern. Repeat until you've created a background effect you like.

Step 11 ... LAYER PAINT WHERE DRESS FORM WILL GO

Mix another complementary color of paint and apply it to the surface with a paper towel. Here, I have an idea of where I'm going to put my dress form, so I want to make that part of the background contrast a bit more with the colors that I painted the clay. To add further texture, spray the surface with your water bottle, let it sit for a few minutes, and then blot the water up with a paper towel (as shown in steps 8 and 9).

Step 12 ... ADD CONTRASTING PAINT WITH BUBBLE WRAP

Brush paint onto a sheet of bubble wrap and imprint it like a stamp on your painted surface. Repeat until you've created a textured effect you like. Here I'm using it to create a darker area near the bottom of my piece.

Stretch Your Wings

Poplar wood is a fine, hard, dry wood perfect for painting on. Always choose good-quality hard, dry wood—otherwise the wood grain might absorb too much of your paint and will warp and bend over time.

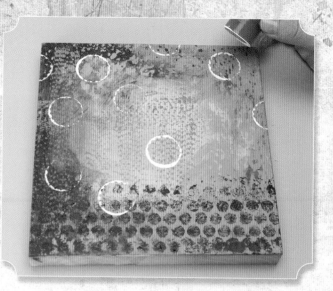

Step 13 ... STAMP WHITE PAINT IN RANDOM PATTERN

Take a small, round plastic lid (I used a shampoo cap), dab it into some white fluid paint, and use it to stamp the surface of your work, brightening it a bit and adding yet another layer of detail. Let it dry.

Stretch Your Wings

If your acrylic paint colors seem too bright for your taste, try using a bit of Golden glaze to mute them. I especially like using Burnt Umber glaze for this effect.

Step 14 ... ADD DETAIL AND DEPTH WITH CHARCOAL

Take a charcoal pencil and trace around the inside of the white stamped circles. Smudge them with your fingers to give this part of the background pattern more shadow and depth. Freehand any other charcoal lines you'd like to further define areas of your painted background, smudging with your fingers as desired. Here, I'm using charcoal to further define the dark, textured area at the bottom of my surface and to add some vertical lines to connect some of my circular areas to the bottom of the work.

Step 15 ... ADHERE DRESS FORM TO PAINTING

Paint the edges of both the baked dress form and the wood black for a finished look. Use extra-heavy gel medium to adhere the dress form to the painted work.

43

"A friend is one to whom one may pour out all the contents of one's heart, chaff and grain together, knowing that the gentlest of hands will take and sift it, keep what is worth keeping, and with the breath of kindness, blow the rest away."
—Arabian proverb

CHAPTER THREE

Creating Community

We all have a story, a life in progress, wanting to be heard, seen, celebrated, lifted up. We are people who feel the creative spirit within, sometimes feeling alone, sometimes struggling to find our way into a group of like-minded souls. Some of us embrace the idea of a creative community, knowing that a collective joy and connection makes us stronger. Some of us shy away from it, worried it would feel too invasive in our quiet lives. Either way, we must acknowledge the truth and understanding that exists when we surround ourselves with a support system.

Whether you're just starting out on your path or you've been creating for as long as you can remember, it's important that you surround yourself with people who are smart, tender and affirming—people who have a solid foundation within themselves to nurture you along your journey while you provide the same for them. Who are these people, you ask? They are kindred spirits who will create next to you, side-by-side, in a spirit of togetherness, without competition. Creative souls who will help you reach for the best parts of yourself and encourage you to fly.

There are many ways to build your own creative community. In this chapter, I'll share my own experience with online communities and how that two-dimensional world spilled over into my real life by helping to create long and lasting friendships with other creative women. I'll also share how moving past our comfort zones and attending art retreats and workshops can often lead us into a creative community we never knew existed. I'll talk about what these experiences look like and how they can inspire us to embrace being a part of a collective creativity. Perhaps you already have a community. This chapter will challenge you to expand its meaning and depth in your life. Regardless of where you are on your path, I hope you'll find what I've found: that these creative connections can have you feeling warm and light, like you're dancing on the sweetness of it all.

• • • • • • • • • • • • • • • • • • •

Opposite page: The Arms of Community, *9" × 12" (23cm × 30cm) mixed-media collage painting on canvas. The background of this painting is a collage of letters, cards and postcards I've received from family members and friends—a sort of tribute to my own community. In this chapter, you'll learn to create your own one-of-a-kind work using this technique.*

FINDING YOUR PLACE

It's autumn outside and I'm having warm and fuzzy daydreams of hours spent in the studio with friends. We would sip on hot tea while we create together, side by side. We would make holiday cards, knit scarves and collage on the wide open floor. There would be joyful messes, music, inspiration and, of course, a good bit of chatting about the latest fabric to debut or a newly discovered line of patterned papers or a painting class we'd love to take at our local art store. While making things, we'd discuss our creative lives, our personal lives, our creative hopes and dreams. Best of all, we'd exclaim, "How cute is that?" as we delighted over our finished creations while planning our next gathering. What I love and envision the most in all of my daydreaming is the idea of being surrounded by creative women who get inspired by the collective energy of being with other like-minded women. It makes my heart still in warmth.

In your own daydreams, what's your place in your community? What's stopping you from making those daydreams a reality? We've all had moments of shying away from other creative souls, hesitant to share our work or our words because we're worried that we're not good enough, that our creativity isn't creative enough. But I assure you, it's never too early in your journey to become part of a group of like-minded individuals. Intimidation can only cause you to miss out on some invaluable opportunities.

Finding our community is essential for our creative dreams to take flight. It gives us the momentum we sometimes need to keep fearlessly leaping toward our creative goals. Whether you are a full-time artist or a stay-at-home mom who loves to create in your spare time, finding other individuals to support you in your artistic endeavors is one the most rewarding discoveries along the creative path. Besides the pure fun that happens when inspired women get together, connections are made over mutual creative sparks. Ideas are born. Dreams are born. Accountability is birthed. The spirit of friendship soars.

Perhaps you already have days like the one I daydreamed about in your very own studio or at a friend's home, where you and your art pals are blissfully sprawled out together on the living room floor with your supplies. If so, then you likely understand that collective energy and spilling of ideas and inspiration I'm referring to. But what about taking the next step and enrolling in that scrapbooking group or knitting circle at your local craft store? Are there areas in your life where you could expand your artistic community?

If you're like me, a bit shy with a tendency to cocoon yourself inside your cozy home, then you'll need to make a focused effort to find your community. Lucky for you (and me), these moments between women, creating our hearts out, loving every minute of our time together, are not hard to come by. It can all start in the comfort of your own home, in your pajamas, on your computer—like it did for me.

EXPLORING COMMUNITIES ONLINE

The Internet is a wondrous tool to get you started in finding your creative community. There are all sorts of artful blogs, weekly online creative challenges, countless mixed-media groups and creative swaps occurring between like-minded people who live all over the country, even the world. These online communities encompass a variety of creative mediums, including knitting, photography, fine art, illustration, sewing and more. It's a large, inspiring world right at our fingertips! And the best part is that there is a bit of anonymity, so the experience doesn't feel as intimidating at first as a physical community might.

When I was just beginning my artful journey and searching for a community of my own, I was especially delighted to discover the large, interactive community of artists and crafters who have blogs. They're like ongoing personal art journals, full of colorful photos, words, creations, ideas. Readers are invited to leave comments—which leave a trail of links to other artful blogs with more color, more art, more inspiration and, yes, more commenters with more links! It's a world of endless interaction, where people (strangers to one another, but creative companions in spirit) encourage one another along the creative path. There are even swaps and collaborations that take place among people who may have never met one another, but who share a common interest in a specific craft and an appreciation for one another's work.

You can imagine my sheer delight when I stumbled upon this discovery years ago. An entire new world opened up for me, and soon, I was posting photos of my own creations on my very own blog while receiving and giving feedback to other creative bloggers. Eventually, I began making connections with artful bloggers in real life—first at cafés, then in our living rooms, or at art retreats. Soon, we were all sprawled out on the floor together, with our supplies and conversation leading the way. Friendships that started online between strangers became very real, deeply nourishing relationships along the creative path.

So, go for it! Try visiting these online communities (I've listed several of my favorites in the resources section on pages 124–125) and start participating in this seemingly unending world of creative inspiration. Perhaps you already have your own blog or belong to an online group that shares ideas. If this is the case, perhaps you could consider reaching out to a fellow local blogger (or two) and arrange a meeting over tea or a trip to the local yarn or art supplies store. Try expanding your online friendships into your physical, everyday world. The support you already feel from your online relationship will be strengthened because of it. Maybe you don't have a blog, but you have a list of your favorites that you read daily. Whatever the case, I encourage you to move past the role of observer and into the role of active participant. If a blog doesn't feel right for you, then try joining a creative discussion group or weekly online art challenge. (Again, turn to the resources section on pages 124–125 for some of my favorites.) You may be surprised at the creative community that will unfold around you as you embrace this uplifting and encouraging world online—and at how easily these experiences can spill over into your daily life.

Soon you'll be crafting with fellow crafters, art-making with fellow artists and taking photos with fellow photographers. And most important, you'll find yourself smack dab in the middle of an uplifting, brave and supportive community that enriches both your life and your creative work. It is possible, my friends. Yes. It. Is.

ATTENDING WORKSHOPS AND RETREATS

I was emotional, the happy kind, the entire trip. Mainly because I knew I had found my community. Finally. It was quite freeing for me.

I wrote this journal entry upon returning home from my first art retreat. Whether or not you are already part of a solid creative community, attending art retreats and workshops is perhaps one of the most gratifying steps you can take toward becoming a part of a richer, more specialized artistic community. These events can quite honestly change your life. You experience something out of the norm of your usual life and remove yourself from outside distractions. You take classes. You learn. You grow. You search. You expand your vision for your life, your creative plans. You find meaning in unexpected places. Best of all, you find a unique gathering of people much like you. People who get excited over the same things you get excited about: a new line of rubber stamps, or a newly discovered way to make a piece of jewelry, or a creative arts magazine that you've been reading cover to cover. This is what creating community should feel like. Supportive. Inspiring. Uplifting. Real and true.

No matter where you are in your path, I joyfully encourage you to push past your comfort zone and attend an art retreat. These are events where workshops are taught by skilled and inspiring teachers. They can be one-day events held in your neighboring town or they can be three-, four-, five-day events held in various parts of the country. There are knitting retreats, photography retreats, mixed-media retreats, you name it. It's a whole other world waiting for you to discover—you may not even have to go very far. Perhaps there is a workshop or retreat being offered just up the road.

It's true that attending an art retreat, whether it's a brief local workshop or a more intensive out-of-state event, can feel a bit daunting. I was scared to death to attend ArtFest, my first ever art retreat. While driving the three hours north to get there, I had worries and concerns about not knowing a single soul once I arrived. In fact, I had feelings quite similar to how I felt the night before the first day of junior high! Would I meet anyone? Where, and with whom, would I sit at lunchtime? How does all of this work? I had many friends in my life, but barely any in the world of mixed-media art and I was eager to make some connections. But still, I was a nervous wreck. Of course, once I arrived, just as I did on that first day of school, I found my place. I engaged. I explored. I got inspired and comfortable with the other attendees. I made friends, and off I went, soaring into the blissful experience that is creating a community.

The truth is that these gatherings of other creative souls can be some of the most affirming and heartening experiences of our lives. We're transported, even just for a day, out of our everyday distractions and errands, and into a world of creative energy and people. Whether you're a full-time artist who experiences the isolation that spending every day alone in your studio can bring, or a young professional pursuing creative hobbies, these events provide an opportunity for creative growth in our lives. The icing on the cake is the creative community that is often born from these amazing (amazing!) experiences.

So, go ahead! Do some research on a few art retreats (local or otherwise) and start planning your big adventure. I've included a list of some popular mixed-media art retreats in the resources section on pages 124–125, but if you're looking for something else, try a quick Internet search on "paper craft art retreats" or "jewelry making art retreats" and follow your creative dreams all the way there. You can do it. Your joyous, understanding, unique and quirky community is waiting for you. My hope is that you find other individuals who get it: who get the collectiveness of it all, who understand the idea that if one of us finds joy, we all find joy.

It's all about finding your place in a community that supports who you are, where you are and where you'd like to go in your creative path. The important thing to remember in all of this is that we are all living, spiritual, creative beings who can soar on the wings of creative friendships with others who are on similar paths. We thrive on experiences and friendships where we feel safe to be ourselves, where we can relate to those around us who might also be experiencing the highs and lows of a creative life. Whether you are shy and reflective or outgoing and lively, there is a community for you.

MEETING MENTORS

No matter who or where you are in the creative journey, you likely have questions. And celebrations. And things you'd like to discuss with someone else until you have an *a-ha!* moment about your creative direction. I don't know about you, but I'm someone who needs a mentor—someone I can look up to, someone I admire, both creatively and personally, and someone I can occasionally go to with a question. These are important people in our circle of creative community, often the backbone of our support.

For me, my mentors are successful, creative women I first met at an art retreat or online. They continue to be generous in answering my questions and listening to bits and pieces of my journey as I sometimes stumble my way through this artful life. They give practical advice, listen and challenge me in ways my closest friends and family cannot. They've also become a few of my biggest cheerleaders as they celebrate and applaud my small steps.

What about you? Who are your mentors? Whether you're a working parent who crafts on weekends and needs a counterpart to help keep you on track, or someone considering taking her creative path in a totally new direction and needing a bit of advice, a mentor can be a guiding force. Mentors are everywhere. Perhaps he's a local artisan whose way of presenting his crafts at boutiques inspires you to be more professional in your offerings. Perhaps she's a fellow fiber artist whom you could contact for help when trying to decipher a complicated new pattern. Perhaps he's an artist you admire who has graciously engaged in an e-mail exchange with you about taking the next step along the creative path. Really, a mentor could be anyone who encourages you along the way and is available to you when you have a question or two.

On the flip side, I believe it's also our responsibility to remain available to those in our creative communities who may be looking up to us. Sure, we can't answer everyone's questions and be emotionally available to everyone who comes our way asking for advice, but we can be good stewards of the creative life. We can gently point someone toward a resource he may not know about or an opportunity she may have overlooked. I find it discouraging that as creative minds, we sometimes compete with one another. We don't support or reach out to those who have sought our wisdom—perhaps out of fear of being left behind, outdone, outcrafted. We get protective of our information and resources, forgetting that someone likely shared their knowledge with us along the way. What is this about? Shouldn't we celebrate art, creative expression and its rewarding journey, no matter who or where we are in the path? This is what it's all about: creating community, being a part of something larger than ourselves. It's important that we not get territorial with our craft. The moment we do this, we let the spirit of community go.

Thank You, Friend, 9" × 12" (23cm × 30cm) mixed-media collage painting on canvas. This painting was inspired by what community means to me: the gathering of like-minded souls who support and nourish one another along the creative path.

Winged Thoughts

To me, a creative community looks like:

_____

_____

_____

_____

_____

When surrounded by supportive and uplifting women, I feel:

_____

_____

_____

_____

_____

I can begin to build a creative community by:

_____

_____

_____

_____

_____

If I had a mentor, I would ask her:

_____

_____

_____

_____

_____

" . . . My friends have made the story of my life." —HELEN KELLER

"Out of the welter of life, a few people are selected for us by the accident of temporary confinement in the same circle. We never would have chosen these neighbors; life chose them for us. But thrown together on this island of living, we stretch to understand each other and are invigorated by the stretching." —ANNE MORROW LINDBERGH

"I never enter a new company without the hope that I may discover a friend, perhaps the friends sitting there with an expectant smile. That hope survives a thousand disappointments." —ARTHUR CHRISTOPHER BENSON

"Thus every man passes his life in the search after friendship." —RALPH WALDO EMERSON

"Home is not where you live, but where they understand you." —CHRISTIAN MORGENSTERN

"I am learning to live close to the lives of my friends without ever seeing them. No miles of any measurement can separate your soul from mine." —JOHN MUIR

"The purpose of relationships is not to have another who might complete you; but to have another with whom you might share your completeness." —NEALE DONALD WALSCH

" . . . Under the magnetism of friendships, the modest man becomes bold, the shy confident, the lazy active, or the impetuous prudent and peaceful." —WILLIAM MAKEPEACE THACKERAY

Rae by my art pal Stephanie Lee, made from plaster, wood, acrylics, a found speaker part, a ceramic bird, acrylic, etched nickel silver and a found bolt. Stepanie says: "Rae is a person who, at first, appears to be standing alone, but upon closer inspection, has a companion. A little bird—light and free of judgment, just watching with quiet, anticipatory support for Rae's next step. Rae is not always certain and sometimes a bit guarded toward the world at large with its boisterous laughter and loud declarations of labels—"I AM IMPORTANT . . ."—but her confidence in herself has grown enough that she is willing to stand tall and be open to the gift of community and all that it brings. Her tall neck, a vulnerable part, is strong and sure, and she gathers herself around her sense of seeing that she has something to offer the world, and she'll do so willingly without requiring the world to reciprocate."

Taking Flight with
CONTRIBUTING ARTIST Stephanie Lee

KRR: Stephanie, you and I have talked a lot about what a creative community means to us. What experiences have led to your feeling more a part of a community?

SL: I have found dear friends online, through teaching and sharing artwork mostly. It is quite interesting to find a kindred spirit in a face you have never seen. These friendships and the support they offer have been instrumental in my creative evolution and in seeing that so many wonderful artists, schooled and self taught, have some of the same exact internal dialogue about their work. This in and of itself (knowing that I'm not the only one) has been the single most powerful influence in my setting those undermining fears aside and working anyway—putting one creative foot in front of the other and seeing what might come of it.

KRR: What sort of struggle or hesitation did you have as you began to build a creative community of support around you?

SL: The biggest struggle for me has been twofold. Number one was feeling interesting enough to draw a creative circle of support around me that would stay the course if I happened to show what I thought was my boring ol' self. I've never been to Italy, and I don't drink fancy wines (or coffee, for that matter), and, frankly, my "dream" vacation includes visions as simplistic as hiking around a new-to-me national park, playing games around a table with friends and family or seeing Alaska by helicopter. Really. Nothing glamorous. I like stacking chopped wood and digging in my garden and especially love "deep" conversations with folks who are full of life and love and creativity (i.e., people like you!).

The second part of this struggle is feeling "creatively adequate" in terms of the physical works I offer. There are still daily opportunities for me to remember that this life of art and creativity isn't a race or a competition. This is all about sharing what we are excited about or feel a need/desire to share for whatever reason, without defining its degree of value, originality or importance. Part of the internal resolution I have found in this area is through observing many a debate about "what is art." When I find myself in a circle of artists (from all walks of life—some with degrees and some without) I find myself hearing every single argument as total truth and valid in its own right.

KRR: Isn't it funny how we all come from a unique perspective, sometimes questioning ourselves along the way, but all coming from the same journey—that of a creative soul. In your heart of hearts, what impact has your creative community had on your path?

SL: More than anything, the shift in creating a community for myself was seeing that it was there—ready, waiting and willing for my acceptance of it. My guardedness kept many wonderful relationship opportunities at bay for a long time, and I didn't offer my fullest, most honest and kind self to anyone for a long time. Through pursuing the work that I love to do, I was connected with others by others who saw something in me that I was overlooking or underestimating. At some point, I decided that I don't need to have all the answers and that perhaps maybe all the little areas within myself that I thought were problematic might not be a big thing after all. I decided to just be open to what another might see in me—to accept that they are drawn to it and to offer whatever I can to that relationship based on that trust.

We often form community because we need support and draw on that, sometimes forgetting what we can offer. I am very clear that I want to close a conversation with a friend leaving them feeling supported, encouraged and uplifted. That is my singular goal in relationships (though, believe me I'm no master at this, by any stretch of the imagination). I am very clear that the kind of community I want to surround myself with is that kind that doesn't revolve around me—where I honestly look at it and gladly have something to offer. In that offering of myself, I find the truest, most loyal and fun support I could ever imagine.

a
charming
friendship.

Learning to Soar

I don't know about you, but I have a habit of saving each and every meaningful card, letter and postcard people give to me. They get thrown in one big pile and often stay there forever. For this project, I wanted to give new life to all those letters and use them as collage bits and pieces in my background. Using personal notes from the people in our lives is a wonderful way to pay tribute to those who give us the gift of community.

The piece I created on the following pages by combining this chapter's contributing artist's techniques with my own is one of my favorites in the entire book because it's chock full of my favorite techniques. After we create a meaningful background, I'll show you how to apply paint and inks to give your collage a distressed but cohesive look. You'll learn how to use your fingers to paint faces with transparent ink—a very simple and fun technique that allows the beloved letters underneath to peek through the skin tones. And I'll share some of my other tips for defining facial features with pens and charcoal pencils. Finally, we'll both learn Stephanie's method of working with plaster to create an embellishment for our painting. Along the way, I'll share my thoughts on what it was like to try out Stephanie's plaster technique and make it my own—a rewarding challenge for me!

MATERIALS FOR CREATING A BACKGROUND OF NOTES AND PAINTING AND INKING A FACE

7" × 7" × 1" (18cm × 18cm × 3cm) block of wood

personal letters/postcards, at least 3

palette paper

Raw Sienna, Titan Buff, Titanium White and blue shades of fluid acrylics

Antique Linen, Tattered Rose and Walnut Distress Ink (Ranger)

Lettuce Alcohol Ink (Ranger)

foam brush

Faber-Castell PITT Artist Pens

white gel pen

charcoal pencil

gesso

gel medium

scissors

brayer

eraser

paper towels

MATERIALS FOR CREATING A PLASTER FORM AND ADDING IT TO A PAINTING

4" × 4" (10cm × 10cm) dry floral foam, about ½" (1cm) thick

Rigid Wrap plaster cloth, about 3" × 3" (8cm × 8cm)

⅓ cup (118 ml) plaster of Paris

words cut from a vintage book

fluid acrylic paints

paintbrush

charcoal pencil

heavy-duty gel medium

gel medium

1 teaspoon (5ml) carpenter's wood glue

disposable mixing bowl

spoon

razor

scissors

water

sparkle glaze (optional)

CREATING A BACKGROUND OF NOTES AND PAINTING AND INKING A FACE

What better background for the subject of your artwork than letters and cards that hold personal meaning? First, I'll show you how to create a cohesive base for your collage—with a splash of color, of course—using a brayer, paint and inks, and then we'll go on to paint and define our subject, allowing the letters beneath to peek through.

Step 1 ... CREATE COLLAGE OF PERSONAL NOTES

Brush a coat of gesso on your block of wood (this will help the paper better adhere to the surface). Cut your letters into pieces and adhere them to the background using gel medium. Keep the composition of your piece in mind when you are positioning your papers. For instance, if you know you are planning to paint a face at the top of your piece, you might not want a paper seam or a very busy letter piece in that area. Finish by covering the surface with a clear coat of gel medium and letting it dry.

Step 2 ... COAT BRAYER IN TWO NEUTRAL COLORS OF PAINT

Place dabs of Raw Sienna and Titan Buff fluid acrylic paints on a piece of palette paper. Run the brayer through the puddles of paint until it's coated.

Step 3 ... ROLL PAINT ONTO THE COLLAGE

Randomly roll the brayer over the surface of the letters, reloading paint as necessary. While the paint is still wet, take a damp paper towel and wipe away little areas of paint to allow the writing to show through. This will give the background a more cohesive look.

Step 4 ... ROLL INK RANDOMLY ONTO THE PAINTED SURFACE

Add some drops of Lettuce Alcohol Ink to the paint that is already on your palette paper. Mixing ink with paint can create some great varied effects. Roll the brayer through the paint/ink puddle again and then roll it over the surface of your piece to add another dimension. Here, I'm keeping my composition in mind and making sure to add more saturated color around the edges. Let it dry.

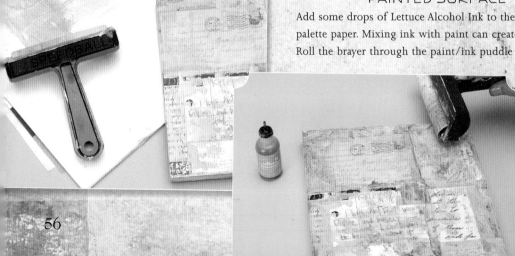

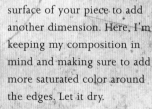

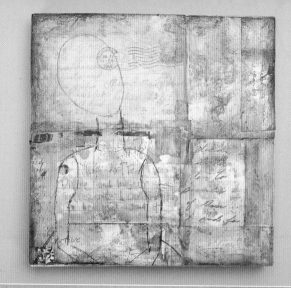

Step 5 ... DISTRESS SURFACE WITH CONTRASTING INK

Rub the Antique Linen Distress Ink pad directly on the entire surface to further give it an aged look. Follow by rubbing the Walnut Distress Ink pad directly on the surface to accentuate edges and give it a burnishing look. Use your fingers to rub this ink in until you've created the look you want, paying careful attention to which letter pieces you don't mind darkening and which ones you'd like to leave more clearly visible. Let it dry.

Step 6 ... PREPARE COMPOSITION AND SKETCH SUBJECT

Use a charcoal pencil to begin sketching the subject you'd like to paint. Have your eraser handy—anything you're not happy with, you can erase as you go.

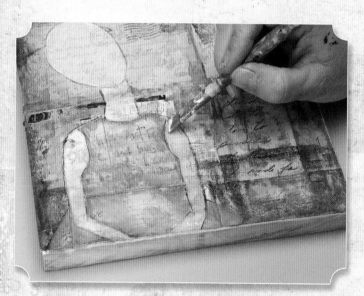

Step 7 ... PAINT SUBJECT

Paint your subject, filling in the lines with a fluid acrylic wash, rubbing the paint with a paper towel from time to time to make sure the letters beneath still show through. If there are any new shades you're introducing, feel free to use the brayer to add a tint of them to the background, as I did with the blue of the subject's outfit here. If your subject has areas that will require flesh tones, as mine does, color them with a very light wash of Titanium White, as I did here. Allow it to dry.

Step 8 ... ADD INK TO PAINTED SUBJECT

Dip a clean finger into the Antique Linen Distress Ink pad and rub it over the entire surface of the face, filling it in with a more natural skin tone. Then, dip your finger in the Walnut Stain and blend it around the side of the face, where a shadow might be, to create a soft, fuzzy look. If any areas seem too dark, use a wet paper towel to wipe a bit of the ink away, then use your fingers to blend it again. Then, use your fingers to apply a bit of Tattered Rose Distress Ink to the cheeks. Use the same technique to add a bit of ink to the arms and neck, emphasizing any shadowy areas with the darker ink. Let this dry.

Step 9 ... DRAW FACIAL FEATURES

With a charcoal pencil, draw in the facial features. Then, use Faber-Castell PITT Artist Pens to fill in the eyes and lips. I like to use more than one color—these pens are perfect for blending. Use a white gel ink pen to fill in the whites of the eyes and a charcoal pencil to further define the features.

CREATING A PLASTER FORM AND ADDING IT TO A PAINTING { Contributing Artist's Technique by Stephanie Lee }

Now we're going to learn Stephanie's method of working with plaster. (As you can see from her incredible piece on page 52, she is an expert at creating unique sculptures with this fascinating medium.) For this project, I employed her technique on a much smaller scale by creating a plaster, heart-shaped embellishment to attach to my final painting. I had never worked with plaster before, but this was a fun exercise to give it a try!

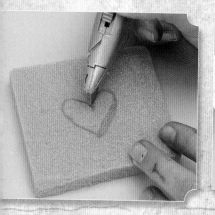

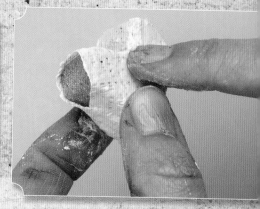

Step 10 ... CUT SHAPE FROM FOAM

Freehand draw a small heart on the piece of dry floral foam. Use a razor to cut out the shape.

Step 11 ... CUT PLASTER CLOTH STRIPS

Use scissors to cut 2 or 3 1" × 3" (3cm × 8cm) strips of dry Rigid Wrap plaster cloth. You'll need enough to cover your piece of foam entirely.

Step 12 ... COVER SHAPE WITH STRIPS

Dip the first strip in water and then wrap it around your foam heart. Rub it around with your finger to cover it entirely with water—you'll notice all the small holes start to blend together with the wetness and the pressure from your fingers. Repeat with the remaining strips until your shape is completely covered. Let it dry completely—about 10 minutes.

Step 13 … MIX PLASTER

Take ½ cup (118 ml) of plaster of Paris and mix it with 1 teaspoon (5 ml) of carpenter's wood glue and a little bit (approximately 1 teaspoon [5 ml]) of water. Mix it very vigorously with a spoon until it is sour cream consistency and as smooth as possible. (If you don't want to ruin your spoon, you'll need to rinse it off right away.)

Step 14 … COVER SHAPE IN PLASTER

Use your fingers to apply the plaster mixture to the Rigid Wrap layer on your shape. You can make the plaster as smooth or as textured as you like depending on how you work it with your fingers. Work quickly—it dries really fast.

Step 15 … PAINT PLASTER SURFACE

Use a paintbrush and fluid acrylic paints to paint the shape the color of your choice. Here, I also added sparkle glaze.

Stretch Your Wings

Here, I used the plaster to create just a small heart shape, but you can make anything from small ornaments to large sculptures using these plaster techniques.

Step 16 … ADD PLASTER SHAPE TO COLLAGE

Use a heavy-duty gel medium to attach the heart to a collage, painting or other work of your choice.

Step 17 … ADD FINAL DETAILS AND EMBELLISHMENTS

Go back over the subject you've painted with the charcoal pencil, emphasizing any lines that may have been painted over or blurred. Use the charcoal pencil to add in some wings and final embellishments. Here I cut the words "a charming friendship" from a vintage book and adhered them with gel medium to the finished painting.

"Listen to your life. See it for the fathomless mystery that it is. In the boredom and pain of it no less than in the excitement and gladness: touch, taste, smell your way to the holy and hidden heart of it because in the last analysis all moments are key moments, and life itself is grace." —Frederick Buechner

CHAPTER FOUR

Finding the Sacred in the Ordinary

In learning to look closely at the moments of our everyday lives, we find abundant inspiration—inspiration that sparks our creative ideas and expression. When we find the sacred in ordinary—a coincidence, a heart-shaped stone or even a sunrise—we allow for a richer saturation of joy and creativity in our lives. Everyday moments become clearer with meaning—moments that we may have never noticed before. And our creative lives are transformed by the inspiration that comes from simply paying closer attention to the abundance that already exists in the ordinary moments of our lives.

Seeking the sacred in the ordinary not only means finding the importance in seemingly unimportant moments within our everyday lives, but it also means acknowledging the value of treasures that are often long forgotten, unused or left behind. My older sister (who happens to be the featured contributing artist in this chapter) does an amazing job of this. Perusing the aisles of junk stores, she finds treasures that may seem forlorn and ragged to some, but she sees their beauty, their sacred meaning. A stack of old weathered books, cracked mirrors, ripped and torn letters—she finds them beautiful in their own special way. And often, they become lovely and engaging centerpieces for her assemblages, where the ordinary becomes extraordinary.

In this chapter, we'll set off on a journey to find the sacred, simple beauty in the things we once thought were unimportant. So, get out your journals, your cameras, your creative spirit, and let's adventure to a place where everything matters and seemingly insignificant tokens and moments suddenly inspire our creativity with their significance.

Opposite page: Time Flies assemblage. Wanting to express the beauty of time and the longings we sometimes have as it passes, I transformed a broken, long-forgotten clock into a meaningful piece of art.

SEEKING SIMPLE BEAUTY

For years, I wondered why my older sister named her creative business SacredCake. I would densely ask, "SacredCake? I don't get it." It took some years of stumbling through my twenties to emerge on the other side with a view and an understanding that there is indeed simple beauty in everything. Everything, including seemingly ordinary things like the falling of leaves, the sweetness of words, the glorious changing of seasons, and yes, even cake. Brilliant. It has likely been one of my biggest lessons learned in life—and it came from my older sister, whose work and wisdom you will see displayed in this chapter. She not only appreciates all the details of everyday life, things you and I might pass over as "forgettable," but she also finds the sacred in everyday materials that might otherwise go unnoticed or be thrown away. She takes these very items and turns them into glorious, meaningful art.

So, what exactly does finding the sacred in the ordinary have to do with a creative life? Everything. Everything. Everything. Finding the sacred in the everyday details not only expands our personal gratitude for every ounce of the world's offerings, but it fuels our creative expression. Once we learn to seek simple beauty, we find ourselves surrounded by inspiration that, when collected inside moments of seemingly insignificant details, expands our creative voice. We see things where we didn't see them before. We pay attention. We get inspired. Suddenly, the sky isn't just the sky. Instead, it's full of shades and shapes we didn't stop to pause and notice before—beauty that may inspire a new project idea. Even raindrops, as my friend Nina has taught me, aren't just raindrops. Instead, they are bubbles of rainwater that, if looked closely upon, reveal a mirror image of their surroundings—how beautiful! Just like the raindrops, inside the casing of our everyday lives are small sacred wonders waiting to be noticed and waiting to spark our creativity. Just as Raoul Vaneigem reminds us, "There are more truths in twenty-four hours of a man's life than in all the philosophies."

DOCUMENTING THE JOURNEY

For me, one of the ways I find beauty and truth in the ordinary is by taking photos of my everyday happenings, of my small discoveries along the way. Some days, I snap photo after photo of treasures I find on my daily walks—the way the sun is setting (reminding me of the birth of possibility and inspiring me to use more yellows and pinks in my paintings), old doorways (signifying so much in their distressed beauty), my feet and shoes (representing literal steps in the journey of life). I also capture images of heart shapes, found in leaves and rocks and wood grain—to me, they represent small and meaningful speckles of universal loveliness and meaning. (Turn the page for a collection of some of my favorites!) All of this photo-taking inspires me to think about how I express my creativity to the world—the colors I am drawn to, the aesthetic I want to capture. It's all right there in my daily life. I just have to pay attention and ordinary things suddenly become anything but.

How about you? Perhaps you're a photographer, already in tune with capturing the small wonders of every day. Is there something you may be missing in the details? Or perhaps you're a mother whose camera has been stashed away, like the china, only coming out for special occasions. What about the special occasion that is today? Perhaps this week you could challenge yourself to carry your camera everywhere. Take a photo of anything and everything that calls to you—your child's colorful stockings, your favorite pair of shoes, the way the light falls onto your skin, the flower that bloomed in your garden today. Pay attention to colors, texture and form, and keep them tucked inside your creative, mindful toolbox. You will be transformed at how much you see and discover. The idea is that these little discoveries will expand your creative vision, perhaps have you thinking of new ideas, new projects, new color combinations and texture. By the way, this is a great opportunity to start that blog or your "whispers evidence" journal (as we discussed in chapter one) or a "sacred things" scrapbook as a way to document your findings. It will help you remember to keep looking, paying attention and celebrating the beauty of the details. Your creative spirit will thank you!

Now that we're capturing our sacred moments in photographs and writing, let's go a step further and start actually collecting physical mementos of our everyday journeys to use in our creative projects. Next time you're on a walk on the beach or in the park, or even while you're window shopping, look for small tokens that call to you. Perhaps it's a crisp autumn-colored leaf or an abandoned piece of weathered wood. Maybe it's your own heart-shaped rock found at the ocean or a handful of seaglass. Think about ways you can use these items in your creative expressions. Could you include your heart-shaped rock in your next piece of jewelry? Perhaps in a sculpture? Could you preserve those few leaves and include them in your next collage? What are some ways you can begin to infuse your sacred-in-the-ordinary items into your work?

In the piece shown here, I used an old, tattered and worn book for my painting. When I found it, I was called to the beauty of its age, its rough edges and the long-forgotten words covering its deserted pages. I thought it would make a lovely and meaningful frame around a painting. This simple, seemingly common and nondescript book now has a new life—it's been transcended from ordinary to meaningful. The idea is the same with the piece shown on page 60. Wanting to express the beauty of time and the longings we sometimes have as it passes, I transformed a broken, long forgotten clock into a meaningful piece of art. The wings, fully inspired by my sister, give it a deeper sense of expressiveness—something that was ordinary before now has a new spirit, a new significance.

Is there anything that you could breathe more life into through a creative project? What about that stack of vintage postcards, or that collection of old buttons, or even your daily photographs depicting everyday treasures? Could they have new life inside a lovely assemblage? Whether you actually use your findings in your creative projects or not, your creative spirit will thank you for beginning to pay attention to the details that hold meaning, to the simple abundance that exists in your everyday life. It's about finding simple significance where perhaps you overlooked it before. It could be the way a stranger opened a door for as you as you entered a busy downtown building. Perhaps it's an understanding glance from friend. Or maybe it's a song lyric that grabs a piece of your soul. Whatever it is, try and capture it—in a journal, in a photograph, on your blog. Your creative spirit will begin to notice these things, too, and your inspiration will soar.

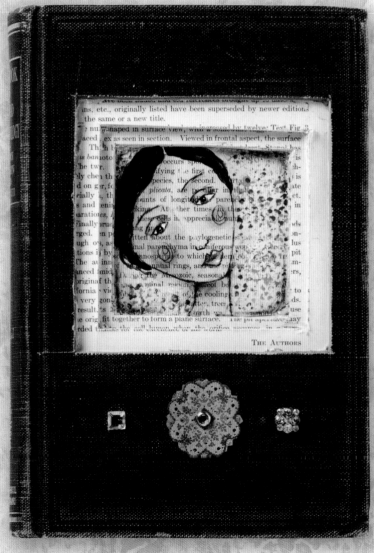

Vintage Book Girl, *small mixed-media painting on watercolor paper framed inside a lovely vintage book. You'll learn how to make your own vintage book frame later in this chapter.*

One of the ways I seek the sacred in the ordinary is by searching for heart shapes out in the world. To me, they represent so much: a message of goodness, perhaps in a very busy day. An unexpected gift that brings on a warm smile. A blessing of hope. The images here are among my favorites. Once you start looking, you'll find that hearts are everywhere: on trees, in the grass, in leaves, in rocks, on the ground, even on an everyday parking meter. I hope you find some of your own, and they cause you to pause for a moment of simple gratitude.

Winged Thoughts

In my everyday life, I may be overlooking things that I want to see
more of, such as:

_____

_____

_____

_____

I find small moments of gratitude at these times, at these places
and/or with these people:

_____

_____

_____

I see beauty in:

_____

_____

_____

I can capture the sacred in the ordinary by:

_____

_____

_____

_____

"How we spend our days is, of course, how we spend our lives. The tragedy is that we ignore so much of it in the interest of getting to the real stuff." —ANNIE DILLARD

"I have found that if you love life, life will love you back." —ARTHUR RUBENSTEIN

"Art washes away from the soul the dust of everyday life." —PABLO PICASSO

"Life never becomes a habit to me. It's always a marvel." —KATHERINE MANSFIELD

"I still get wildly enthusiastic about little things. . . . I play with leaves. I skip down the street and run against the wind." —LEO BUSCAGLIA

"Gratitude is the memory of the heart." —JEAN BAPTISTE MASSIEU

"Again and again I've taken quick glances and then for some reason . . . it's opened up like one of those Japanese flowers that you put into water and something I thought wasn't worth more than a casual, respectful glance begins to open up depth after depth of meaning." —SISTER WENDY BECKETT

"All of us are watchers—of television, of time clocks, of traffic on the freeway—but few are observers. Everyone is looking, not many are seeing." —PETER M. LESCHAK

"How fortunate we are to make our life's work centered on experiencing life with depth and creating a soulful response to it." —LINDA SACCOCCIO

sacred

Sacred assemblage by my talented sister and contributing artist, Jennifer Valentine. In this piece, Jennifer communicates the message that we are sacred and beautiful souls, imperfections and all.

Taking Flight with
CONTRIBUTING ARTIST Jennifer Valentine

KRR: Jennifer, you have taught me so much about thinking twice about my everyday surroundings. Can you tell me how finding the sacred in the ordinary has inspired your creativity?

JV: My creativity is inspired by everyday objects that most people overlook or regard as useless items. In looking closer at things, I experience them in a way that one would witness a life. For instance, when I use a mirror in my work, I think of the life it has had, the faces it has seen, the places it has been, and when it was finally rendered useless . . . and then, somehow, it finds me. I rescue these discarded lives, and each object tells me its own special story. In my work, I marry the various objects together to tell a unique and meaningful tale. Sacredness comes when I can look deeper into the meaning of objects and turn it into an experience.

KRR: I appreciate your being so mindful with your art-making—it becomes about a meaningful experience, not just for you, but for those who are called to it. Tell us about your signature wings, like the ones in *Sacred* (shown on the opposite page). They grace many of your pieces. What is the significance for you?

JV: The significance of the wings is a symbol of escape, freedom and divinity. For this piece, the wings symbolize the freedom and clarity that comes when we realize that, with all of our imperfections, each of us is a sacred being.

KRR: Tell us about what this lovely mirror piece means to you. Does the mirror reflect an inner knowing, a reflection of some kind?

JV: Imperfection inspires me to create. The mirror piece is very meaningful to me. A positive self image can be abolished by our own negative inner voices. The constant glare of the media says we have to look a certain way in order to achieve acceptance and beauty. This mirror piece communicates the message that we are sacred and beautiful souls, imperfections and all. It reminds me of my own divinity and sacred self.

KRR: What is your advice for those who desire to seek more of the sacred inside a seemingly ordinary life?

JV: Seeking the sacred in the ordinary is mindfulness that can be practiced moment by moment. When you open yourself to all of the goodness that life has to offer, even the simplest activity can become a sacred event. In the perceived ordinariness of our lives, there lies potential. Even if we feel depleted and unable to find joy, the simple idea that we are given this day may be enough to begin the process of finding divinity in our lives.

KRR: Can you give me a recent example of an everyday moment in your life that held more meaning once you looked more closely?

JV: Just the other day I was examining a beautiful autumn leaf and I experienced such childlike wonderment. Suddenly, I found the universe there. How can something so simple yet so complex be an accident?

Learning to Soar

I've long admired Jennifer's winged creations, so it was such a joy for me to learn exactly how she makes them in adding them to this vintage book photo frame project. My mind went haywire with creative ideas. I could add these simple-to-make but deliciously distressed wings to just about anything—paintings, assemblages, vintage picture frames, boxes and on and on.

First, I'll show you how to turn a vintage book into a lovely photo frame, transforming an everyday item into an extraordinary centerpiece for a craft project. Then, we'll learn Jennifer's technique for making a set of those gorgeous and delicate wings out of tissue paper and wire. Adding them to our book will create a whimsical and meaningful work of art. So come along with me as we find our creative wings (literally!) and transform something ordinary into something more.

MATERIALS FOR CREATING A VINTAGE BOOK PHOTO FRAME

old hardcover book

photograph

decorative chipboard letters (K&Company)

3 buttons or other embellishments

foam brush

pencil

gel medium

glue stick

straightedge

sharp razor blade

3 bulldog clips

fine-grit sandpaper (optional)

MATERIALS FOR CREATING WINGS

about 40" (102cm) 22-gauge wire

white tissue paper

sparkle glaze, or gel medium and loose glitter

Walnut Stain Distress Ink (Ranger)

foam brush

heavy-duty gel medium

setting mat

hammer

heat gun (optional)

CREATING A VINTAGE BOOK PHOTO FRAME

When I was younger, my mom taught me how to make photo frames out of old vintage books. I've been making them ever since, adding my own touch and embellishments, and I'm thrilled to share a bit of my family's creativity with you in this project inspired by both my mom and my sister. All you need is a simple book and a favorite photo.

Step 1 ... TRACE POSITION OF PHOTOGRAPH

Position a photograph where you would like it to appear through the front cover of the book. Use a pencil to trace the outline of the photograph onto the cover. If the area you want to frame extends toward the edges of the photo, you'll want to trace an area at least ¼" (6mm) around the edges of the photo instead of tracing the photo itself, as some of the image will be covered later.

Step 2 ... CUT OPENING IN COVER

Take a sharp razor blade and, using a straightedge, cut along the pencil lines, pressing hard enough to cut completely through the cover. You may need to score over the same line multiple times with the razor before it cuts completely through the hard cover. Erase the pencil lines if they are still visible.

Step 3 ... DRAW SMALLER SQUARE INSIDE COVER OPENING

Using your pencil and straightedge, draw lines to form a smaller square inside the area you just cut out from the cover. Here I drew a square about ½" (1cm) smaller than the first one, but yours can be any size you like.

Step 4 ... CUT OUT INNER LAYER OF THE BOOK'S PAGES

Open the flap and line up your straightedge with the first line of the inner square. Use your razor to begin cutting through the interior pages of the book. You can apply a lot of pressure and score the line several times for a deeper shadow-box effect, or apply lighter pressure to create a shallower frame. Remove the cut-out centers of the pages. You may have to play with this a bit to get it even, cutting more as necessary.

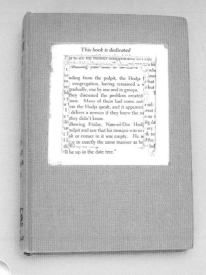

Step 5 ... CHOOSE A PAGE TO BE THE VISIBLE TOP LAYER

Once you have the inner square cut out, page through the first few pages and see if there is any writing you'd like to expose as your top layer. Here, I found the words "This book is dedicated" just above my cut-out square a few pages into the book, so I ripped the first few pages out of the book until this page was the top layer.

Step 6 ... DRAW AND CUT A THIRD SQUARE WINDOW

Use a straightedge and a pencil to draw another square inside the first—this will serve as yet another layer of your frame. Mine is about ¼" (6mm) inside my first cut square. Repeat the process of scoring the lines with your razor and straightedge and removing the inner portion of the pages, cutting as deep or as shallow as you like.

Step 7 ... ADHERE PHOTO IN FRAME

Position the photo inside the frame so that the portion of the photo that you want to frame peeks through the inner square. Use your glue stick to adhere it in place.

Step 8 ... EMBELLISH COVER

Use a glue stick to adhere some decorative chipboard letters, vintage buttons or other embellishments to the cover beneath or around the photo frame.

Step 9 ... SEAL EDGES

Using a foam brush, apply a heavy coat of gel medium to the edges of the pages to seal the book closed (don't worry if you're messy—it will dry clear). Clip a bulldog clip to each edge of the book to hold it tightly together as it dries. Put any finishing touches on your piece that you'd like. Here, I peeled back a bit of the cover around the window that's been cut to create a more distressed look.

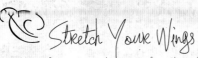

Stretch Your Wings

Use a fine-grit sandpaper to fray the edges of your book if you want to enhance its distressed, vintage look.

CREATING WINGS { Contributing Artist's Technique by Jennifer Valentine }

Now for one of my favorite contributor techniques! We're going to put our book photo frame aside while we try Jennifer's unique way of making a lovely set of wings out of wire and tissue paper. Remember, the possibilities are endless. You could make these as small or as large as you'd like, and add them to just about anything—think of your favorite old clock or a decorative vintage bottle. Have fun with it!

Step 10 ... CREATE BASIC WIRE FORM

Fold the ends of the wire inward until they meet. Twist the ends together in the center to hold them in place, forming a sort of figure eight. Protecting your work surface with a setting mat, use a hammer to pound the center twist flat.

Stretch Your Wings

Use any kind of tissue paper you want for your wings. Old sewing patterned tissue paper is one of my favorites for creating a unique, vintage look.

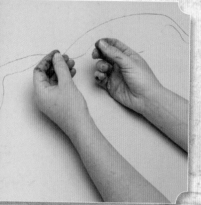

Step 11 ... SHAPE WINGS

Use your hands to shape the two circles of the wire figure eight into the shape of wings, making them as symmetrical as possible.

Step 12 ... ENCASE WINGS AND PAPER IN GEL MEDIUM

Lay the wings on a piece of white tissue paper cut to be slightly more than twice their width. Use a foam brush to totally encase the wings and the surrounding paper in gel medium. It's OK if the tissue paper gets wrinkly, but be careful not to tear it—it can be fragile once moistened by the medium.

Step 13 ... FOLD AND ADHERE PAPER

Fold over the tissue paper and press it firmly into the gel medium, sandwiching the wire wings. Let it dry completely. (You can speed this process up a bit by using the heat gun, if desired.)

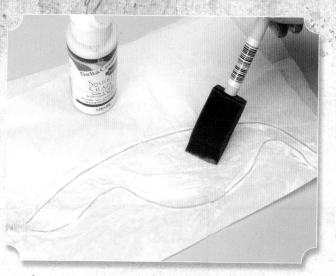

Step 14 ... COAT WINGS WITH SPARKLE GLAZE

Brush a sparkle glaze over the surface of the wings with a foam brush (or brush gel medium onto the surface and then sprinkle it with glitter). Let it dry completely.

Step 15 ... DISTRESS PAPER SURFACE WITH INK

Rub the Walnut Stain Distress Ink pad gingerly over the surface of the tissue paper to give it a more antique look and to emphasize the lines of the wire. At this point, it's very important that you let the wings dry completely before moving on to the next step.

Step 16 ... REMOVE EXCESS PAPER

Very carefully tear the excess paper away from the edges of the wire to expose the shape of the frame. Be sure to leave the wire encased in the tissue, tearing the tissue only outside of the wire form.

Step 17 ... ATTACH WINGS TO VINTAGE BOOK PHOTO FRAME

Use a dab of heavy-duty gel medium to secure the wings in between some of the pages in the bottom right corner of the photo square. Or you can attach the wings to another project of your choice.

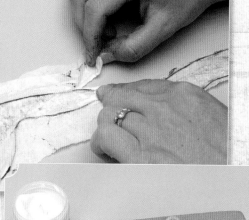

Stretch Your Wings

If your wings seem too translucent, you can add a second layer of tissue paper with gel medium.

"Painting is not a means of communication or even self-expression, but rather a process of discovering, or uncovering."
—Louis de Brocquy

CHAPTER FIVE

Honoring Memories

Whether you are a sculpturist, collage artist, painter or graffiti artist, making art is healing. It gives us an outlet to express our fears, our joys, our hurts, our love—regardless of whether we intend it to. It's all right there in our subconscious, some of it recognizable and some of it not. The meditative practice of making art allows our hearts to expand, think, even forgive. This is especially helpful to those of us who struggle with expressing ourselves verbally. Through the process of exploring our creativity, we communicate with color, brushstrokes, collage. Our spirits soar on this expression and our lives feel more peaceful, calmer.

In this chapter, we'll explore how we can honor our memories through making art—how we can pay tribute to the person we were while becoming more of the person we want to be. We don't have to be grounded or held back by our past; we can indeed take flight into a space of honoring our joyful memories while at the same time healing old hurts and disappointments.

We'll also explore how the process of creating allows us to communicate what may be difficult with verbal expression. How the end result, whether it's a finished painting or collage, isn't always the most significant part of our creative expression, but in fact, it's the very process of falling into a creative zone that provides the real healing for us. So, grab your journals and your supplies and come with me into a space of personal and expressive growth as we spread our creative wings.

• • • • • • • • • • • • • • • • • •

Opposite page: Sweet Memories, 9" × 12" (23cm × 30cm) mixed media on canvas. This piece honors my childhood memories of my older sister and me. Here we are, framed in the chest of a girl who is expressing simple and sweet healing of a childhood that has long passed. Later in this chapter, I'll show you how to create faces with paint and sandpaper, as I did here, as well as how to add meaningful photos to your artwork.

> "When our eyes see our hands doing the work of our hearts, the circle of Creation is completed inside us, the doors of our souls fly open, and love steps forth to heal everything in sight." — MICHAEL BRIDGE

EMBRACING LOST MOMENTS

Like our art, our memories are deeply personal. Memories, both joyful and painful, blend into our everyday lives and shape us into who we are today. Have you ever thought about how who you were in years passed affects who you're becoming now? Perhaps you're where I was before I experienced the healing powers of art—so resistant to allowing difficult memories to define who you are that you don't acknowledge their impact on your life today.

By trying to keep the hard stuff of our lives at bay, we never quite allow ourselves the opportunity to sit with the hurt, own it, then move past it. We fail to realize that pain needs to be expressed so that the person we were meant to be has room to breathe, to grow and to become. Creativity can be that release we need. For me, it wasn't until I discovered my art that I really began to sit with all that I needed to and allow the breath of life to filter out the pain of what I needed to take with me and what I needed to leave behind on the journey of who I was becoming.

Of course, I didn't expect this to happen. I thought I was just having fun getting my hands covered with glue and paint! But over time, I felt a release of old wounds and an expression of new joys. I consider it a happy accident that I, in many ways, pay tribute to many of my past experiences and memories while returning to (and becoming) the person I was meant to be. Simply creating did this for me, and it can do it for you, too!

In chapter two, I wrote about getting back to our eight-year-old selves—fearless, creative and bold. For me, this means getting back to the spirit of the child I was before losing a parent to a tragic car accident—getting back to that playful spirit before trauma entered my life. Making art has been the healing force that has helped me recover my eight-year-old spirit, my relationships, my life. This doesn't mean that I'm replaying the trauma of losing a parent with every painting. It just means that I am, in some ways, paying tribute to a life unfolding, of all that I didn't have control over and of the life that has been waiting for me all of these years. With each painting, whether it's conscious or not, I'm returning to who I was meant to be. I am honoring my life, the life of my parents, and all those present in my life, both in spirit and in flesh. It's the most expressive healing I can imagine, this outward reflection of a life in progress, this returning to the childlike wonder that exists in all of us.

I have a dear friend, Mati Rose, who also lost her father at a very young age. In art school, her critiques were often quite painful as she struggled to agree with her teachers and acknowledge that perhaps her childlike yet sophisticated paintings were a deep response to all that she had lost as child. As the subconscious became conscious, so did her healing. And her art, by the way, is lovely and amazing (you will see it in the following pages). In many ways, Mati has learned to paint with an expressive and youthful freedom that comes from honoring all the bits and pieces of her life and memories.

How about you? Do you notice your inner child coming out to play when you're being creative? Have you noticed that you feel calmer, more reflective, more in a position to heal, when you make your art? Collage, for instance, can be a wonderfully therapeutic and meditative medium. By putting together images that speak to you, you are, in some ways, having a conversation with parts of your heart and soul that are yearning to be expressed—a seemingly insignificant image in your collage piece may, in fact, mean much more to a small piece of yourself that was once kept deep inside a pocket of your heart. Each work of art is another opportunity to acknowledge and express all that is a part of ourselves, past and present, and perhaps allow a small space of growth and healing.

HEALING THROUGH EXPRESSION

Sometimes, however, healing through art doesn't have to be kept and expressed in the subconscious at all. Rather, it can be quite deliberate and fun. For example, not too long ago, my older sister, Jennifer (who you met in chapter four), sweetly sang a song into my voicemail that I had long forgotten. It conjured up a whole flood of lovely memories because it was a song she used to sing to me whenever I had trouble falling asleep as a young child. In response to this, I made the piece "Sweet Memories" (see page 76). I copied an old photo (one that captures the images of us inside the

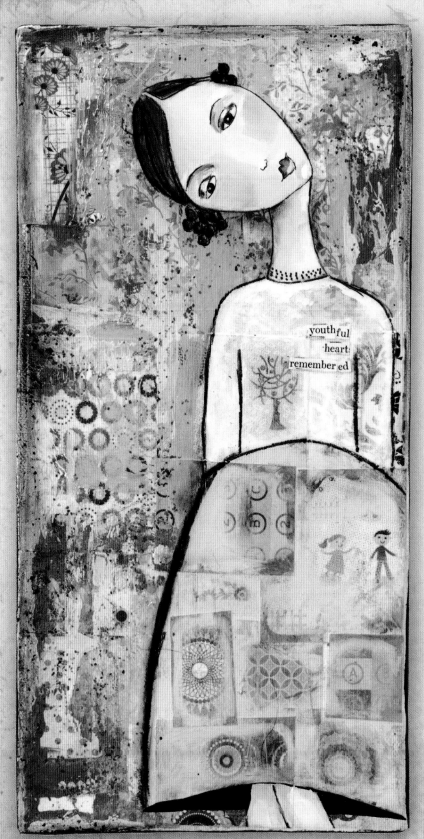

youthful
heart
remembered

Youthful Heart Remembered, 6" × 12"
(15cm × 30cm) patchwork collage painting
on canvas. My intention was for my subject
here to be remembering her youth, how it felt
to be wild and free and creative. Slowly, she's
learning how to let her youthful heart shine
again, to come out and play in creative bliss.

memory I was having) and positioned it in the chest of the subject. I wanted to give her a somewhat youthful appearance, hence the childlike hairstyle. But I also wanted to give her a face that was somewhat weathered, representing a well-worn, well-loved and well-traveled spirit. In this piece, I'm honoring my older sister and all she gave me in those years: comfort, laughter and protection. I'm also honoring a memory, a moment I wanted to capture.

Are there creative ways that you can deliberately take yourself into your memory through art? Are there photos of you or your life that you could use in your artwork? Scrapbooking and art journaling are wonderful ways to honor our memories. They're outward artistic expressions of lives blossoming in the here and now, evolving from one day to the next, capturing our memories in colorful detail and design. In the world of mixed-media art, I see a ton of artwork using vintage images of strangers. How about using images of yourself instead?

Or how about writing a poem, making a photo collage or writing an art journal entry about whatever it is that is calling you to remember? Here's another idea: Think about all the trinkets and ephemera that represent something about yourself. Why not use them in your artwork as a means to express who you were and who you are today? You might choose to include an image, a few words clipped from your childhood books, or a vintage necklace that reminds you of your beloved grandmother. Whatever your craft, your life (past and present) wants to be expressed, to have a space and place to feel invited to release, to grieve, to rejoice, to heal.

My friend Mati Rose does a wonderful job of using physical bits and pieces of her life in her art. A piece of lace that belonged to her grandmother, a photo she cherishes from long ago, a few lines from a poem she wrote in college—all this and more finds its way into her pieces. In the end, her paintings reflect an honoring of her memories and her everyday life spilling over into her creative life. It's inspiring, this healing and expressive tribute to the things that matter in our hearts, souls and memories.

Another favorite artist of mine uses meaningful phrases and photographs of her favorite places and people—the tree she played under as a child, the farmhouse she once lived in, the oak-lined street where she played with her siblings—in her jewelry (protected under resin). These creations pay tribute to all that she's lived while resonating with her customers who find value in meaningful jewelry, where personal images and words come together to create a story. I love this idea of blending ephemera, both old and new, into our artistic creations.

LOVING THE PROCESS

Whether our work is a direct response to a specific memory or a collective celebration of a life in progress, making art is undeniably a way to express our everyday ebb and flow of feelings, a therapeutic way to release whatever emotional space we may have come from, or may be in at this very moment. I know many people who aren't able to effectively verbalize what they're experiencing emotionally, but through their art, they're able to beautifully express their language in color, in symbols, in line. Whether it's a doodle, a scribble in an art journal or a painted masterpiece, the idea is to communicate your hopes, your dreams, your wishes, your hurts.

Sometimes, the end result, the finished project itself, isn't the most significant expression of healing. Instead, it's the creative process that is therapeutic—picking up the pencil and drawing, cutting paper and gluing a collage, mixing colors with a paintbrush. It's the creative process, the exploration of our artistic selves, that allows us to grow. It unites our spirits, minds and bodies until we become whole again. It's a spiritual rebirthing, this healing that occurs when we allow our spirit to express everything it needs to through the creative process.

So get out your paper, your paint, your clay and begin to explore your self, your memories, the paths of your heart. Don't worry about the end result. Through the process of expressing your creativity, you may find yourself, perhaps without even trying, more resolved in your heart and in your life. Lighter. Freer. Soaring on the wings of self-expression.

Remember, 8" × 8" (20cm × 20cm) mixed media on canvas.
*She's lost in joyful memories of a collection of experiences
that make her who she is today. Like the collage bits in
the background, her memories, like a puzzle, fit together
perfectly to give her a foundation to build on.*

Winged Thoughts

In my creations, I intentionally wish to express:

In my artwork, my subconscious mind seems to be expressing:

After spending some alone time creating, I feel:

I can deliberately express my life—past and present—in my art by:

"Forgiving does not erase the bitter past. A healed memory is not a deleted memory. Instead, forgiving what we cannot forget creates a new way to remember. We change the memory of our past into a hope for our future." —**LEWIS B. SMEDES**

"The primary benefit of practicing art, whether well or badly, is that it enables one's soul to grow." —**KURT VONNEGUT, JR.**

"We do not remember days, we remember moments." —**CESARE PAVESE**

"You will learn to enjoy the process . . . and to surrender your need to control the result. You will discover the joy of practicing your creativity. The process, not the product, will become your focus." —**JULIA CAMERON**

"I think that one's art is a growth inside one. I do not think one can explain growth. It is silent and subtle. One does not keep digging up a plant to see how it grows." —**EMILY CARR**

"There is no art without contemplation." —**ROBERT HENRI**

"Painting transports me into another dimension which, quite literally, refreshes parts of the soul which other activities can't reach." —**PRINCE CHARLES**

"This is where creativity, intellect, experience and passion for nature merge into artistic discovery. Memory plays a huge part in composing paintings that speak to this and I am encouraged by the strong role this plays in my work." —**GAVIN BROOKS**

Honoring Grammie Hillman, 12" × 12" (30cm × 30cm)
mixed media on wood by our soulful contributing artist
Mati Rose. In this piece, Mati pays tribute to her beloved
Grammie Hillman in an honest and expressive painting.

Taking Flight with
CONTRIBUTING ARTIST Mati Rose

KRR: You have such a tender story about how you came into your creative life. Can you share a bit of that?

MR: I have always been a maker and dreamer, but it wasn't until recently that I called myself an artist. My dad was an artist and died in a car accident when I was only a year and a half. Growing up, I connected to my father through the art that he made and left behind. I learned about him by studying his woodcuts and sculptures and deciphering his doodles in his notebooks. Very early on, the lesson of art as a tool to communicate was instilled upon me. I am so grateful that he was an artist and left these gifts for me to behold. Furthermore, that he passed on his creative genes and impulse to create.

KRR: Has art been healing for you?

MR: It has been tremendous for me to discover how art heals and mends. Sometimes it's how I think of my creative process—I put down a lot of randomness and then try to "heal" it by making sense and beauty of it. Initially, I thought that I wanted to be an art therapist because I understood how art could heal oneself and it sounded like a practical way to pursue my interest in art. I spent several years facilitating art workshops, first with prisoners and then with homeless children. . . . It wasn't until I looked deep inside myself and figured out that I really wanted to focus on being the artist (and not the facilitator of the art), that I felt most healed, and then able to give back in the form of pictures and happiness and connection to others.

I am often working from a place of memory, childlike wonder and exploration, and that sometimes does bring up sadness because I'm connecting to that little girl who is grieving. Other times I just want to paint an elephant!

KRR: Do you think, in some ways, you rediscover your youth through your paintings?

MR: Absolutely! I feel like the best state of painting and creating is when you are playing and open to possibilities. Just like when you're a kid. I also think, as children and adults, we are working out our lives through this play and, in some cases, escaping to this place of possibility that allows us to problem solve and dream through our [art], that then we can apply to our lives.

KRR: Tell us about this lovely collage painting.

MR: I spent a lot of time with my Grandma Hillman (I called her Grammie) when I was younger. She was my dad's mom, and after he died, we lived with her for a bit. She was a former teacher and crafty lady and let me wreak creative havoc with costumes, building blocks and cutting up my Papa's socks to make puppets. The collage is a tribute to my Grammie Hillman and the wings that she passed on to me, along with her actual sewing kit, which you can see from her "Handmade by" label.

KRR: Do you have any advice for people who are trying to infuse their memories into their artwork?

MR: I think this is an excellent place for people to start when they are uncertain of what to draw or paint. You can start by brainstorming different memories, large and small, silly and significant: Think of your favorite song as a fifth grader or your grandfather's aftershave as you hugged him or even your dream last night—and then try to describe your memory of it in paint. Would the memory have wobbly lines? Is it fast and expressive? What color would the memory be? I think you can push it even further when you try to narrate your memories and actually paint the lyrics of that song by Madonna and incorporate that brown couch with the little afghan pillow on it that your parents had when you did interpretive dance in the living room, etc. Collage is an excellent medium for incorporating memory because you can include actual artifacts, such as a fabric pattern or photo. Art has no rules and is all about expressing yourself through free association and connecting the dots to the past and your present, so anything you put down is valid and authentically you.

Learning to Soar

OK, so now we get to play and let that childlike energy and spirit lead the way. First, we'll both learn Mati's technique of using a vintage sewing pattern in a collage background. Carefully chosen pieces like this that hold special significance for us can infuse meaning into our work, even if only we know it's there. We'll take this a step further by using Mati's technique of creating a spray-paint resist with vintage doilies or other ephemera—a subtle but colorful technique that you can easily adapt to your own style.

Once we've established a background rich in texture, I'll show you my techniques for creating a somewhat weathered but sweet face using paint and sandpaper. I'll also share some of my favorite ways to add finishing touches, including the use of gel pens, glazes, ink pads and ephemera. And you'll learn how you can honor an important part of yourself in your artwork by incorporating a treasured photo into a painted collage. I chose an image of me and my momma, and I so enjoyed combining my own techniques with Mati's in a finished piece that truly shows it off.

MATERIALS FOR USING SEWING PATTERN PAPER AND CREATING A SPRAY-PAINT RESIST

7" × 7" (18cm × 18cm) block of poplar wood, about 1" (3cm) thick

sewing pattern paper

patterned papers

3–4 doilies (plastic, paper or fabric)

spray paint in two coordinating colors

foam brush

gesso

gel medium

MATERIALS FOR ADDING A PHOTO TO A PAINTED COLLAGE

photograph

picture frame embellishment (Wild Asparagus)

decorative button

"Family" brad (K&Company)

black acrylic paint

Walnut Distress Ink (Ranger)

black Faber-Castell PITT Artist Pen

white gel pen

charcoal pencil

fine-grit sandpaper

gel medium

glue stick

MATERIALS FOR CREATING A FACE WITH PAINT AND SANDPAPER

rhinestone bezel

Titanium White, Burnt Sienna, Burnt Umber and Raw Sienna heavy-bodied Golden acrylics

fluid acrylics in various colors

Tattered Rose Distress Ink (Ranger)

gesso

small paintbrush

fine detail paintbrush

white gel pen

charcoal pencil

fine-grit sandpaper

charcoal blender (optional)

Raw Umber glaze (optional)

heat gun (optional)

USING SEWING PATTERN PAPER AND CREATING A SPRAY-PAINT RESIST

{ Contributing Artist's Technique by Mati Rose }

Learning Mati's techniques and using them for this part of the project was so fun for me. I love how the sewing pattern and spray-paint resist (using doilies—how fun!) helped to create a vintage wallpaper-inspired look.

$\mathcal{S}tep$ 1 ... CREATE COLLAGE AND COAT WITH GEL MEDIUM

Gesso the surface of your block of wood. Use gel medium to adhere a variety of pieces of patterned papers to create a vintage-looking background. Here I used pieces of a flower-patterned scrapbook paper, a vintage piece of map and a sewing pattern. Finish by brushing a coat of gel medium over the entire surface. Let it dry.

$\mathcal{S}tep$ 2 ... CREATE SPRAY PAINT RESIST WITH DOILIES

Lay a few doilies onto the collaged surface to act as a resist. Spray paint a light coat of paint over the doilie—don't worry about applying it evenly at all. Then spray paint a light coat of the coordinating color over another doilie. Remove the doilies to reveal the resisted pattern. Let it dry.

CREATING A FACE WITH PAINT AND SANDPAPER

This idea was born from a happy accident: I was trying to sand away unwanted layers of heavy paint from a subject's face that I wasn't happy with, only to discover how much I loved the weathered beauty of the sanded face! This is a wonderful, not at all intimidating way to paint a face—and to completely let loose and have fun. There are no mistakes with this very forgiving technique.

$\mathcal{S}tep$ 3 ... SKETCH SUBJECT

Use a charcoal pencil to sketch your subject on the painted surface of your work.

Step 4 ... LAYER SKIN TONES OF PAINT IN FACE AREA

To create this face, we're going to layer skin tones of heavy-bodied acrylic paint and then sand them away to create an even, blended surface that appears weathered. Start by applying a layer of gesso on the face and neck area of your subject to create an opaque base. Then blend Titanium White, Burnt Sienna and Raw Sienna heavy-bodied Golden acrylics and apply a thick coat of the mixture to the face and neck area. Let it dry a bit, or give it a quick blast with a heat gun.

Step 5 ... LAYER DARKER PAINT IN AREAS OF SHADOW

Add a bit more of the Burnt Sienna and a little bit of Burnt Umber to your mixed paint. Apply the darker color to one edge of the face, where the shadows might rest, and to the cheek areas and eyebrows. When using this technique, I always start with the shadowy areas first, and then work my way to the lighter areas.

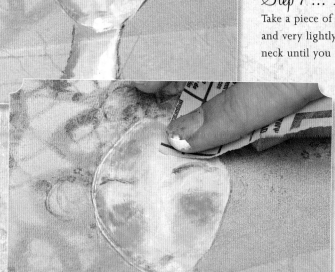

Step 6 ... ADD WHITE PAINT TO HIGHLIGHT AREAS OF LIGHT

Apply some Titanium White thickly to areas where the light might rest. I'm targeting the bridge of her nose, a bit of one side of her forehead, and areas near her eyes, chin and forehead. The effect should be splotchy and uneven; don't worry if it looks messy—in fact, it should. Let it completely dry before moving on to the next step.

Step 7 ... SAND LAYERS OF PAINT

Take a piece of very fine-grit sandpaper (the finest grit you can find) and very lightly begin sanding the heavy layers of paint on the face and neck until you get the blended effect you want.

Stretch Your Wings

Sewing patterns are great background papers because they establish a nice sepia tone for your work, giving it a more vintage flair.

Step 8 ... DRAW AND PAINT FACIAL FEATURES

Use a charcoal pencil to draw in fine-detail lines for the facial features—eyes, nose, lips, eyebrows and hair line. Blend the lines with a charcoal blender to soften them a bit if you want to. Finish the face by using a detail paintbrush to color in the lips and eyes and a white gel pen to add detail to the whites of the eyes.

Stretch Your Wings

If you don't like the effect that is blended and revealed after the face is sanded, go ahead and start layering the paint onto the sanded surface, and start the process all over again. You can do this as many times as you want to until you create an effect you like.

Step 9 ... ADD FINISHING TOUCHES TO SUBJECT AND BACKGROUND

Paint the hair with fluid acrylic paint and use the white gel pen to add highlights and give it some definition. Then use fluid acrylics (here, I mixed a few shades with a Raw Umber glaze) to color in the dress with a transparent hue so all the beautiful layers beneath show through. Use a soft charcoal pencil to redefine any lines that have been painted over (here, I outlined the figure) and add any embellishments (here, I added a belt). Use a white gel pen and a rhinestone bezel to create a necklace. Lightly rub a Tattered Rose Distress Ink pad over the surface of the dress and the background to highlight the wrinkles in the tissue paper, giving the piece an aged, crackled look.

ADDING A PHOTO TO A PAINTED COLLAGE

Lastly, we'll add a meaningful photo and other embellishments to your painting. My hope for you is that you will, in the end, have a painting that holds meaning to you and that you'll treasure always.

Step 10 ... SELECT, CUT AND DISTRESS PHOTOGRAPH

Choose a photograph you'd like to include in your painting, and cut it down to a small size. Use a fine-grit sandpaper to distress the glossy surface, particularly the edges. You can be as subtle or as dramatic as you like.

Step 11 ... ADHERE PHOTO AND FRAME

Adhere the pre-made picture frame embellishment to the photo using a glue stick. Adhere the framed photo to the painting with gel medium, then sand the edges of the frame (to blend it with the background) and the inside edges of the frame (to blend it with the picture). Use a charcoal pencil and a bit of Walnut Distress Ink to emphasize the structure of the frame.

Step 12 ... COMPLETE PAINTED, EMBELLISHED COLLAGE

Add finishing touches to make your piece cohesive and complete. Here I added darker distress ink around the edges, used a white gel pen to add embellishments to brighten the skirt and added a brad with the word "family" to give the piece a bit more meaning (this photo is of me and my mom, after all). I finished by adding a button to serve as a photo hanger and some dots drawn with a black Faber-Castell PITT Artist Pen to transform the framed photo into a wall hanging. Finally, paint the edges of the wood with black acrylic paint.

CHAPTER SIX

Speaking Our Truth

We all have our truth. Some days our truth looks optimistic, pure. Other days our truth feels burdened, complicated. Through our creativity, we can express these truths and explore more of what we were meant to discover within ourselves. In this chapter, we'll see how each and every creation we make is a small, telling step in our journey leading to the bigger truth of ourselves. Each piece of art is an opportunity to reveal more of who we are today—and of who we are becoming.

We'll explore what it means to embrace our vulnerabilities as they relate to our creativity. When we allow ourselves to be honest about where we are— creatively, emotionally and spiritually—we begin to nurture a truth inside us that may want to be revealed. We can do this in our art making. Embracing our vulnerabilities doesn't show weakness. Rather, it simply reveals honesty and truth about what's in our hearts; it gives our creative wings the freedom to discover what's ahead.

Infusing our work with our intensely personal truths, whether our approach is secret and softly subtle or literal and triumphantly loud, empowers our creative spirits as well as the spirits of others who are on similar paths. I hope you'll learn how expressing where you are in your journey today can empower a sense of freedom within you. Give your creative spirit permission to create with abandon, with a free-spiritedness that comes from telling the truth as you know it.

• •

Opposite page: Truth Seeking, 8" × 10" (20cm × 25cm), mixed media on canvas. *This painting is about the journey of seeking one's truth, something we are always striving toward in our work. Later in this chapter, I'll show you how to create a patchwork collage painting similar to this one and to add interesting texture with molding paste, as I did here.*

EMBRACING OUR VULNERABILITY

I read somewhere once that pain is the difference between what you are and what you want to be. Isn't that the truth? That inner turmoil we feel sometimes, when we intuitively know something isn't quite right in our lives, is its own sting, its own little pain. It is what motivates us to continue to change and grow and learn our way to our always evolving truth. What is so beautifully alive about this idea is that we can share, inside the meaning of our craft, the spaces between where we are and where we're going. Each creation is an expression of our truth today.

Regardless of our craft or art form of choice, some of our best work can come from a place of vulnerability, of being open to the burdens and even the joy in our lives, then releasing it all. So often, people think that to be vulnerable means that we're weak. That we're emotional. That we're inviting hurt. No, that's not it at all, really. Instead, we can approach our own vulnerabilities as a way to empower our truth, the parts of ourselves that want to be expressed, then released. Are we feeling thankful? Let's show that in our work. Are we feeling overwhelmed? Let's express that, too, even if it's through the process of creating rather than through the actual creation. Creativity is an expression, much like talking, seeing, feeling. Just as in any other means of expression, we can tap into our vulnerabilities, embrace them and create deeply meaningful work that will connect with the deepest parts of ourselves and others. Embracing our vulnerability creates a moment in time for us to get really honest with ourselves, both in our creative lives and our personal lives. Once you express this in your creations, your personal life will feel lighter. You'll feel the weight of a burden releasing itself. Why? Because you've created a healthy and meaningful release of its expression in your work.

Sometimes when I'm creating a painting, something uncomfortable gets dredged up for me. I feel awkward, restless, in ways that I can't quite put my finger on. Through the process of sitting down at my table and putting paint onto paper, this is what happens: I nurture that very vulnerability that had me feeling uncomfortable in the first place. It gets released. I feel freer. I often add words to my paintings to express what it is I'm nurturing in that very moment. Phrases like "tell your story," or "silent emotion," or "unbroken wings, discovered," are all bits and pieces of my own vulnerability peeking through in my art. It not only makes the process of making art more meaningful to me, but also creates an invaluable connection with other women who are also struggling or working through similar issues. It's sending the message that it's OK to speak our truth. It will be heard.

How can you express your vulnerabilities? Remember that being vulnerable doesn't mean you have to share your secrets. It just means owning what you have to own, wherever you may be in the journey of your life. This can be happiness, sadness, gratitude, confusion or even joy. Whatever the case, it's about nurturing and expressing something that needs attention in your life. For me, sometimes this means paying more attention to all that is good in my life. Other times, it means honoring a soft, broken piece of my past. Sometimes this is obvious in my artwork, sometimes not. A large part of it comes through in the actual process of sitting down for a few hours and painting. At the end of the day, I can see what I've expressed in the finished painting, whether it's clear to anyone else or not.

Expressing your vulnerabilities doesn't have to be a public artistic expression. Perhaps it's creating an art journal where you can privately and quietly reveal and work through your truths. Perhaps it's writing your own memoir, just for you to read. Perhaps it's a lovely necklace that you made just for yourself that only you know the deeper meaning behind. The idea, whatever direction you take, is to embrace what's going on inside your heart—your questions, your fears, your loves, your uncontainable joy. Get it out there in writing, in collage, in scrapbooking, in journaling. It will empower you to keep seeking, to keep growing, to keep finding meaning in your vulnerability and truth.

Remember, embracing your vulnerability is simply being honest. Say what it is you really want in your life and also where you stand today. Say it. Express it. That's all you have to do to honor the truth that lies inside your heart. After that, the universe will gently take it, dreams and hopes, burdens and pain, and bring to you all you could ever need.

TELLING OUR STORIES

In the spaces between who you are today and who you are becoming lies a truthfulness, a unique sensibility, that if expressed in your creations will document your life in progress while making a deeper, more meaningful connection with those who view your work. It's true. You have a story to tell. You can tell it quietly in the nuance of your conversations and creations, or you can tell it boldly. Either way, by sharing part of yourself, you're honoring where you stand today while seeking your truth as you become more—more whole, more honest, more of yourself—as you learn to dance and reach and grow toward the best parts of yourself. Your art wants you to dig deeper, to seek your truth, to share it.

Here's a real truth: We are all already whole. We are enough right where we are today, in spirit, in creativity. We are enough—where we stand in this moment, in this life, in this body—as beautiful, messy and confusing as it may be. Let's talk about it. Let's express it. Let's create it. Let's be real and honest and truthful about where we are today and where we hope to go. It's possible to express all of this in our art, whether it's journal making, painting, beading or quilting. The finished work may not have an obvious truth, but you will have created a deeper meaning and will have spoken more intimately to those along the way who see your creations or hold them in their hands and feel the connection—the universal yet personal message you have expressed.

Occasionally, I'll get an email from a friend or colleague expressing disappointment that nobody seems to be purchasing their work. "I really tried to think about what other people would want to buy, and I'm a bit disappointed as to why my pieces aren't selling," they'll say. To me, trying to make artwork based on what we think others might want is just one of the many ways we cover our truth. I say make the art you want to make. Make it meaningful to you. Use colors and elements that you are in love with. When you do this, you'll speak your truth, sharing your own unique vision with the world. Nobody else would have created it the way you would have created it. Try not to worry about what you think other people would like, because chances are, they'll respond more to your truth more than to your assumption of what they might or might not want.

How, then, can you deliberately express more of your personal truth in your creations? The first step is to acknowledge what it is you're trying to express. If you're not sure, try revisiting some of the things we tapped into in earlier chapters. Are you feeling called to express a newly revealed whisper, or a fear, or maybe even a joyful memory? Perhaps you'd like to express a newfound insight you've discovered by seeking the sacred in the ordinary. Or maybe your creative truth simply wants to express sincere gratitude for its reawakening.

If you're still stuck, try thinking about the last piece of art you saw that really tugged at your soul. What was it about that piece that struck you? Could the answer be something you'd like to express in your own creations? If you're still struggling with acknowledging what personal truths you'd like to express, then try answering the prompts on page 98. The act of putting your thoughts in writing may get your creative spirit thinking of new ways to express itself. Whatever the case, it's important to draw your truth from your vulnerabilities and your inspiration. What is influencing your work at this very moment? What is inspiring you?

For example, if you've been deeply influenced by your natural surroundings, perhaps you can create meaning in your collage work by infusing bits and pieces of nature in your creations. If this has symbolic truth for you, if it's a personal message of how nature has nurtured your journey, then it will connect with someone else in a similar way. Perhaps you are more literal by nature, and express yourself best plainly, in no uncertain terms. You might include a narrative quality to your pieces, adding your own words to your artwork, whether embedding a favorite line from a poem inside a jeweled bezel or incorporating journaled thoughts in the depths of your multi-layered painting.

Or perhaps you'd feel safer if your meaning isn't obvious to the viewer at all, but limited to a bond exclusively to you and the chosen recipient of your work, or even placed in the protective hands of the collective spirit of the universe. This doesn't mean you can't still find a way to express your truths artistically. For example, I have a dear friend who fashions the most lovely totes out of wonderfully colorful fabrics. What's so meaningful and truth-telling about a tote, you ask? Each one comes with a tiny fictional story, a narrative journey of what she hopes to express with that item. The stories resonate with every woman who longs to wander fresh fruit markets, or fields of flowers, or Parisian streets—all with her lovely tote in hand. The little story created a meaning, revealed a tiny bit of

new, the quiet beauty of a weed popping through an everyday sidewalk crack. My hope for you is that you, too, insert your own truths of everyday life into your work. Perhaps you can begin simply. Try adding something personal and meaningful to your next collage, even if it gets covered up with other materials in the end. Perhaps it's a letter to yourself, a meaningful song lyric jotted on a pretty piece of paper or a copy of your favorite poem. Or try stitching a personal memento within your next quilt. It may be enough for you to simply know it's there. When you share part of yourself—of your truth—in your work, it touches down into a meaningful part of you, the creator.

The point is to express our truths as we know them today, to let our vulnerabilities show in our work so that we personally acknowledge an important part of ourselves, but also so that people will respond with real emotion. They'll see their own story in our stories that have been expressed in our art. Telling the truth does this for us all, whether we realize it or not. Getting the contents of your heart out into the world is good. It's healing. And it's honest.

Veramente, 9" × 12" (23cm × 30cm) mixed media on canvas. In Italian, "veramente" means "in truth"—the exact expression I was hoping to convey in this painting.

the creator's truth, and made a connection with another woman—all without sharing that truth with the casual observer.

I have another friend who makes lovely necklaces. They're quite simple in their beauty, but the best thing about wearing them (besides the lovely colors of the beads) is that she blesses them before she sends them out into the world. That simple notion, a little meaningful story or blessing, creates meaning for her as well as for me as the recipient of her work. It's all about connection, about expressing our truth with others who can relate. People respond most passionately to work that speaks to them, whether it's in a soft whisper or in a scream.

I've always found that photographers are quite good at capturing the subtleties of life's truth—the splash of a puddle in autumn, the wide grin on a child's face as he discovers something

Free, 9" × 12" (23cm × 30cm) mixed media on canvas.
This painting expresses the freedom I feel when I allow
my vulnerabilities to show, when I embrace them with a
knowing that they can empower me to seek my truth.

Winged Thoughts

Today, my truth looks like:

_____
_____
_____
_____

To me, embracing my vulnerabilities means:

_____
_____
_____
_____

I am called to an art or craft that expresses:

_____
_____
_____
_____

In my artwork, my heart wants me to express more:

_____
_____
_____
_____
_____
_____

"The better the artist, the more vulnerable he seems to be." **—A. ALVAREZ**

"When we were children, we used to think that when we were grown-up we would no longer be vulnerable. But to grow up is to accept vulnerability . . . To be alive is to be vulnerable." **—MADELEINE L'ENGLE**

"An artist feels vulnerable to begin with; and yet the only answer is to recklessly discard more armour." **—ERIC MAISEL**

"Those who are willing to be vulnerable move among mysteries." **—THEODORE ROETHKE**

"It is a choice we artists make, that is not too unlike love, where we find ourselves venturing into a realm of total vulnerability. . . ." **—KIRK WASSELL**

"If I create from the heart, nearly everything works; if from the head, almost nothing." **—MARC CHAGALL**

"For me, painting is the endless quest to find the moment of truth. I'm still working on it. Aren't we all?" **—CHERYL CRISS**

"Do your thing and I shall know you." **—RALPH WALDO EMERSON**

"Making art is about finding the true self—not who everyone has told you that you are, but the person you are truly." **—BIRGIT O'CONNOR**

UNBURDENED

Unburdened, 12" × 12" (30cm × 30cm) oil painting on canvas by ever-inspiring contributing artist Christine Mason Miller. In this painting, Christine expresses how our creative spirit soars on the unburdened wings that come from living a life with truth and honesty.

Taking Flight with
CONTRIBUTING ARTIST Christine Mason Miller

KRR: Christine, you are someone whose truth and honesty spill out into just about everything you do. How have you learned to express this in your work? What motivates you to speak your truth in life and in art?

CMM: The main turning point in my life with regard to living by and speaking my truth was the year I went through a divorce and my soon-to-be ex-husband was diagnosed with stage IV Hodgkin's lymphoma. It was a year that included some of my darkest days, but also enabled me to grow more fully into my own skin and become more aware of how important it was to live honestly at all costs. To me, living honestly is about being honest with myself first and foremost—being aware of my own issues, insecurities, fears and blocks and recognizing how I contribute to frustrations in my life. I find honesty to be incredibly liberating, because in the glow of its bright light, there is nowhere to hide, there are no others to point my finger to for blame, and all I need to do is face the truth, accept it, learn from it and then move on.

I express this in my work by trying to push myself further than I think I can go. I have lately been drawn to the notion that nothing is too precious, that a painting I did last week has value just for the experience and even if I like it, the better idea might be to paint over it and see where it takes me next. It is about letting go of attachments and being willing to release something that might be pretty comfortable or pleasing, but could be much more vibrant and alive if I let it go or maybe even destroy it.

I should note that my ex-husband is now fine and participating in triathlons, after having miraculously beaten cancer less than four months after his diagnosis.

KRR: When I first laid eyes on your oil painting *Unburdened* (shown on the opposite page), I felt a connection to it. I instantly felt a rush inside my own heart in knowing that capturing then releasing our truth really can have us feeling freed. In painting it, were you trying to express a personal truth at the time? Are you always conscious of what you're expressing in your creativity, even if it's just a representation, a small step in your journey?

CMM: I tend to start creating without a clear vision of what I will ultimately finish with. I work on multiple pieces at a time, and the message within each piece emerges as I work. There are a lot of layers in my work, and the more layers I do, the more what I want the piece to say begins to come forth. I have to dive in, keep working and let the piece tell me where it wants to go.

KRR: Do you have any advice for someone in the creative process who may be wanting to express their truths in their art but might be struggling with tangible ways to do it?

CMM: The best advice I can give is to, as much as possible, be willing to push any creative endeavor as far as you can. There are times when I know I could say a piece is finished and I could be happy with it, but I try not to say anything is final until I know I've tried everything, even at the risk of messing up something I like and having to go in an entirely different direction. Be willing to mess up or even destroy what you are working on to get the best, most authentic work out of you. The greatest creative joys I have are usually when I try new directions that feel risky for whatever reason.

Learning to Soar

For this project, I wanted to incorporate Christine Mason Miller's skillful use of oils and gold (as seen in her gorgeous painting on page 100) into a project that also used some of my own favorite techniques. But equally important, in this painting, I wanted to express the idea of having faith that if we believe in ourselves, we can soar—perhaps with a set of our very own golden wings. This was my little piece of truth that came through in this piece, my intention behind the painting. So, come along with me as we embrace our creativity and create a painting that has heart and your very own truth.

I'll share with you the secrets of creating a patchwork collage background that we'll paint in later steps to reveal a fun and unique patchwork painting, an effect you see in many of my paintings throughout this chapter. I'll also share with you unintimidating ways to work with oil paints (specifically for the face). Inspired by Christine's work, we'll then add in a little bit of gold to the wings. And finally, I'll show you how to use molding paste to create interesting texture—another of my favorite techniques that is demonstrated in most of my paintings throughout this chapter.

MATERIALS FOR CREATING A PATCHWORK COLLAGE

7" × 7" (18cm × 18cm) block of poplar wood, about 1" (3cm) thick

various patterned papers

foam brush

charcoal or graphite pencil

gesso

gel medium

MATERIALS FOR WORKING WITH OIL PAINT STICKS AND GOLD LEAF

sheet of gold leaf

words cut from a vintage book

Shiva Artist's Paintstiks in assorted colors

black oil pastel

fluid acrylics in various colors

palette paper

paintbrush

fine detail paintbrush

pencil

black fine-point Faber-Castell PITT Artist Pen

white gel pen

Stabilo black pencil

graphite pencil

liquid gold leaf adhesive

gel medium

fine-grit sandpaper

paper towels

MATERIALS FOR ADDING TEXTURE WITH MOLDING PASTE

light molding paste

bubble wrap

black oil pastel

fluid acrylics in various colors

palette paper

gesso

paintbrush

brayer

paper towel

CREATING A PATCHWORK COLLAGE

There's nothing I like more than cutting up some of my favorite patterned papers and gluing them down to create a colorful, patchwork collage. In later steps, you'll see the transformation from plain collage to painted patchwork.

Step 1 ... GESSO WOOD AND SKETCH SUBJECT

Gesso the surface of the wood. Sketch your subject with pencil on the white surface. For this piece, you'll need to decide upon your composition and draw your subject first, because you'll be building the patchwork collage inside the lines you've drawn.

Step 2 ... BEGIN PATCHWORK COLLAGE

Cut small pieces of patterned papers and arrange them inside the area you want to collage. Here I'm filling in the area of my subject's face as well as the area of her skirt. Choose a focal point image—here I'm using a butterfly—and include that in the composition, as well. Adhere the papers with gel medium and finish by brushing a coat of gel medium on top. If you've covered up your pencil lines, sketch them back in once the gel medium is dry.

ADDING TEXTURE WITH MOLDING PASTE

Working with molding paste is super easy, and I love how it lends interesting effects and texture to a piece.

Step 3 ... APPLY MOLDING PASTE TO SELECT AREAS

Molding paste is useful for dramatic building of thick layers and texture. Use your fingers (or a knife, if you want a smoother texture) to spread a thick layer of the molding paste over an area where you would like to add texture to your piece. Here, I targeted the area at the bottom left of my subject and created some circular swirls in the upper background area, as well.

Step 4 ... IMPRINT BUBBLE WRAP INTO MOLDING PASTE

Press your bubble wrap, textured-side-down, into the molding paste, applying firm and even pressure. Pull the bubble wrap back to reveal the texture you've created. Let the paste dry completely.

Step 5 ... APPLY PAINT WITH BRAYER

Gesso the facial area. Select or mix 2 colors of fluid acrylics (I chose pale blue and yellow). Roll a brayer gingerly through puddles of the paints on your palette paper and roll it over the textured area of your work surface—it will color the raised areas and highlight the bubble wrap imprint. Brayer other background areas, being careful to stay outside the lines of your figure. Let it dry.

Step 6 ... ADD DEPTH WITH OIL PASTEL

Unwrap an oil pastel (I'm using black) and slide the length of it over the surface of the molded areas to further emphasize the texture.

Step 7 ... PAINT OVER PAPERS

Use a paintbrush to apply a thin layer of fluid acrylics over the patchwork paper collage that makes up the dress. Smudge or blend it with a damp paper towel to better reveal some areas, such as your focal point (the butterfly here) until you create the effect you want. Use your brayer to add a bit of the colors you used in the skirt to the background for a cohesive look, as I did here with the red.

WORKING WITH OIL PAINT STICKS AND GOLD LEAF

Inspired by Christine's work, we'll incorporate gold into our project. I have to admit it's a color I would normally run from, but I really love how it turned out in this painting. Continuing with Christine's inspiration, we'll go on to work with oil paints—one of my all-time favorite ways to paint an expressive face.

Step 8 ... DRAW WINGS AND ADD ADHESIVE

Use a pencil to sketch the shape of your wings over the background. Paint liquid gold leaf adhesive inside the lines of your wings. Let it sit until the milky appearance appears clear—usually about an hour. (It will still feel tacky to the touch.) We will fill in the wings with the gold leaf after the mixture turns clear (see step 14).

Step 9 ... SAND AREA TO PAINT

Sand the gesso-covered face area to create a smooth surface for the oil paints. Shiva Artist's Paintstiks are oil paints in stick form that I love using to paint faces. (Thank you, artist and friend Misty Mawn, for introducing them to me!) They're great because they dry in 24 hours, are nontoxic and can be blended with traditional oil paints. Start by going over the face area with Titanium White and blending it with your finger to create a thick base layer.

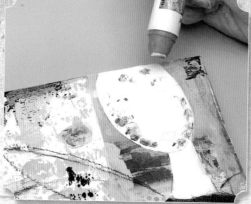

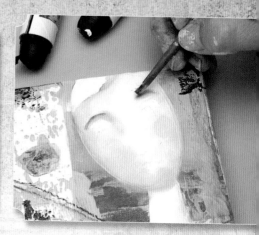

Step 10 ... ESTABLISH FACIAL FEATURES

Use a pencil to make indentions in the paint where you want your eyes, nose, mouth and hairline to be. I don't paint my hair with oil paints, so once I've drawn the hairline, I'll wipe away the oil paint in the hair area.

Step 11 ... ADD OIL PAINT SKIN TONES

Dab on the Yellow Ochre paint all over the face area. Do the same with the Burnt Sienna, focusing on the sides of the face, which will be darker than the middle. Apply dabs of Raw Umber on the side of the face that will have the most shadows and in the eyebrow areas.

Stretch Your Wings

You can also trace a stencil onto your canvas and apply metallic leaf to that area to create a very defined embellished area, as Mati did with the silver bird images in her piece on page 84.

Step 12 ... BLEND AND REFINE PAINT

Use your finger to blend the skin tones together, working from the edges in. Wipe off your finger with a clean, dry paper towel periodically to prevent blending darker hues into areas you don't want them. Add more paint as needed to get the effect of natural skin tones. (I added a bit of Alizarin Crimson to the cheeks with my pinky.) Dab a detail paintbrush into the black oil stick and into the Raw Umber and mix them on palette paper. Use this shade to paint the eyebrows and blend them with your fingers. It's OK if you bleed the paint right over your penciled-in features. They were meant to be guide-lines. You can better define these areas with pen after the oil paint dries.

Step 13 ... DEFINE PAINTED FEATURES

Decide which areas of the face need more definition. Here, I blended brown shades of oil paint around the eyes, white across the forehead and down the bridge of the nose, and rose to the cheeks, then extended the skin tones down into the neck. Work

and blend with a small detail paintbrush or your fingers, whichever is more comfortable for you. Let the paint dry for 24 hours (sometimes it may take longer, depending on the humidity).

Step 14 ... ADHERE GOLD LEAF

When the gold leaf adhesive turns clear, you are ready to add the leaf itself. Press a sheet of gold leaf firmly over the adhesive area. Be careful to stay clear of the wet paint on your face.

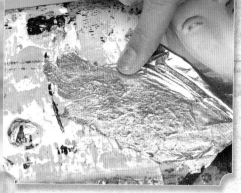

Step 15 ... REMOVE EXCESS GOLD LEAF

Use your fingers to slough the excess gold leaf off of the areas that were uncovered by the adhesive to reveal your wing shape. Be careful not to slough off the gold leaf onto your wet oil paint.

Step 16 ... ADD OUTLINES WITH PENCIL AND OIL PASTEL

Use a Stabilo black pencil to outline the wings and to add any definition that you'd like them to have right on top of the gold leaf. Use a wet fingertip to blend the pencil lines to soften them. Use the black pencil to outline the dress, smudging here and there with your wet finger. Also, use a black oil pastel to highlight the edges of your painting to give it a burnished look.

Step 17 ... LET DRY, THEN ADD DETAILS

Make sure your oil-painted face is completely dry. Use a black fine-point Faber-Castell PITT Artist Pen to outline the eyes, nose and mouth. The pen should write easily right over the dry oil. With a white gel pen, add further accents and brighten areas that could use a bit of a highlight, such as the golden wings and the inside of her eyes.

Step 18 ... COLOR FACIAL FEATURES

Use a detail paintbrush and some fluid acrylic paint to color in the mouth and the eyes. Use a white gel pen to add highlights to the lips and to draw in the whites of the eyes. Draw in hairlines with a charcoal pencil, then colorize the hair area with fluid acrylics. Outline the face and neck with the black Stabilo pen to give them a bit more definition.

Step 19 ... ADD FINISHING TOUCHES

Finish by using gel medium to add a few meaningful words cut from a vintage book as a final touch on the patchwork skirt.

Stretch Your Wings

When you let oil paint dry, be sure to put the work in a cupboard or another clean, enclosed space so that dust particles cannot settle in the oil.

"...Try to love the questions themselves as if they were locked rooms or books written in a very foreign language. Don't search for the answers, which could not be given to you now, because you would not be able to live them. And the point is to live everything. Live the questions now. Perhaps then, someday far in the future, you will gradually, without even noticing it, live your way into the answer."

—Rainer Maria Rilke

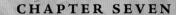

CHAPTER SEVEN

Embracing the Journey

The creative journey comes with a myriad of questions. "What should I do next?" "What exactly is my style?" "Am I doing it right?" So often, we rush toward the answers because not having concrete resolution makes us anxious, worried. But here's the real truth: So often we sabotage our creative growth by providing an often temporary and swift answer to a question that wasn't ready to be answered. The creative life isn't about quick answers or reaching the destination. It's about the journey, often led by our very questions—a life in the making, in progress, questions and all.

In this chapter, we'll explore the idea of embracing not only our questions, but the struggles of the creative journey, the inevitable ups and downs. We'll discuss ways we can acknowledge all the aspects of our creative flight, good and bad, and remind ourselves that it's okay to feel disappointments, bliss and exhaustion—sometimes all in the same week!

We'll also talk about how sometimes it's in the not knowing whether or not we're on the "right" path that we gain the most clarity and freedom to explore our creative spirit. After all, there are no cookie-cutter experiences when it comes to living the creative life. We don't have to necessarily know and control every step along the way. Our creative spirit is asking us to let go, to embrace the idea that all moments are key moments in the big picture of our creative lives.

So come with me as we take flight into acknowledging and validating everything that comes our way in this unique adventure of living the creative life!

Opposite page: Life in Progress, mixed media on an old kitchen cabinet. I painted this piece as an expression that we can very much feel connected to our lives as they unfold, even if we don't have the answers along the way. It's OK. We are enough. Later in this chapter, I'll share techniques for using stamps and other household objects to create texture, as I did in creating this piece.

LEARNING TO ENJOY THE JOURNEY

Sometimes the creative life feels like a wild adventure, complete with the constant ebb and flow of bliss-filled moments, tangled-up emotions and an endless sea of questions. Often, it's the questions that take up an enormous amount of emotional space in our creative lives. Feeling slightly anxious, we may rush toward the answers, thinking they'll bring peace and knowing. After all, our creative voice, though instinctively unique, is still attuned to the world we live in—a world of quick solutions, easy answers, fast-paced technology and concrete explanations. Naturally, we seek instant answers, not realizing that perhaps the questions want to stay awhile, get nurtured and patiently stroll their way toward resolution.

The questions of our creative journey follow every move we make. They ask, "What should I do next? Should I try teaching workshops? How about licensing?" Or maybe they sound more vague, like, "What kind of artist am I? Do I want to continue along this path? How do I know if I'm even on the right path?" If you're like me, you may get so involved in seeking the answers to these kinds of questions that you forget you don't necessarily need to know the answers today. Sometimes, it's in the not knowing that we gain the most clarity. Just as Rilke suggests, we must try and live the questions inside our hearts, honor their existence, sit with them for a while and nurture what it is they are trying to teach us. After all, there lies great mystery and potential inside the spaces of the very questions we sometimes rush to answer.

Likewise, some of us avoid the questions altogether. We just follow our paths, perhaps feeling a bit uninspired, yet we stay the course, keeping the status quo. This is when we really need to start having that conversation with our creative spirit and asking questions—because questions, even without knowing the answers, expand our creative curiosity and potential for growth. So, go ahead and ask the questions! By asking them in the first place, we may trigger or unearth a buried whisper—something we explored in chapter one. Asking questions like "What is it I really want to do?" or "How can I feel more saturated with joy in my creative life?" are wonderful ways to start engaging your creative spirit.

Embracing the questions that pop up along the creative path means engaging in a dialogue with them, similar to any heart-to-heart you would have with a dear friend—one where you would be completely engrossed in what they had to say, nudging the conversation along with an understanding glance or two. Just like a friend

in need, your questions don't need you to offer an easy solution. They just want to be heard and validated. The answers will come later, in small, unforced moments, perhaps when you least expect them. It's in the journey, after all, where our creative truth and answers breathe and live and dance—not in the planning and the plotting and the seeking of a destination.

Creatively, this means being mindful of the opportunities that lie camouflaged in our unasked or unanswered questions. Maybe there isn't a next step right now. Maybe you don't have to know if you're on the "right" path at this very moment. Sometimes, our creative spirit wants us to express what it means and feels to be in the very moment we're in today instead of anguishing over the ins and outs of where we're going. Perhaps the questions are really asking us not to know, not to control, not to immediately answer away their wisdom. Instead, they want us to embrace them, hang out for a while, without a task-oriented to-do list with a straight and narrow trail that leads to "the answers."

Like so many others, sometimes I think I need to know the exact direction I'm heading. My practical, organizational nature takes over and begins to micromanage every step of my creative journey. Perhaps you're like me, a taskmaster, who likes to feel in control of her surroundings, her creative steps. The spreadsheets come out. The calculator comes out. My analytical brain gets excited and ready to work, work, work. What I have learned, over and over again (the lesson keeps repeating itself until I finally get it), is that I don't have to know exactly where it is I'm going to land. Rather, it's the journey, the beautifully fluid and organic nature of the creative process that is the most important and rewarding, not the destination. I can let go of the "what ifs" and the "shoulds," because here's what I've learned: When we're doing what it is we're meant to do, when we allow our creative spirit a bit of freedom to roam the mysteries of the "unknown," the universe opens up to us. We don't worry over the details. Things seem to serendipitously fall into place. We are in the moment. And our creative spirit soars.

The wonderful part of embracing the questions of our creative lives is the creative abandon it gives our spirit. Once we rest with the knowledge that we don't have to know, then we begin to understand that all we have to do is our best, and the rest isn't ours to determine. In essence, we just have to show up. Show up with our paints, our hands, our creative energy and our curiosity, and simply do our best. The rest isn't ours to control. The answers lie in the simplicity of having faith in the journey.

Remember that it's OK to stay in a space of unknowing for awhile, to just sit with the questions themselves without knowing an immediate answer. And even at times when your inner voice is shouting all the answers, remember to keep your inspired curiosity nurtured every step of the way. One of the most important parts of the journey is to dig deep, to ask the questions in the first place and to give a voice to all that is inside of our hearts.

GROWING DOWN THE CREATIVE PATH

I'll be the first to admit that embracing the questions while trying to live in the moment can cause all sorts of emotional upheaval. Keeping the balance is difficult. The truth is that as we grow creatively, so does everything else in our lives and hearts. We feel growing pains, the stretching of our creative souls out of their comfort zones and into seasons of rebirth. This affects every aspect of our lives— our relationships, our creativity, our daily routine. But through all of the pushing and pulling,

we eventually find our way to a place of calm, where our creative spirit can soar on all that it has learned—even if what it has learned is that it doesn't have to know where it's going. We all have creative growth spurts—they're born from the friction we feel inside, the sitting with the unanswered questions and riding the wave of the creative journey until the answers find us. It's all a part of the journey.

Perhaps you've noticed your own pattern of haphazardness in your creative life lately— the waves of emotion, the thrills, the disappointments, the arrivals and departures of

Unleash Your Creative Spirit, 9" × 12" (23cm × 30cm) mixed media on canvas. This piece honors reflections and affirmations that accompany me on the creative path.

111

inspiration, the vague feelings of gratitude that everything is raw and beautiful—often accompanied with a longing. We all have our fair share of rough patches along the way. The creative life isn't always an easy one. There's solitude. Rejection. The constant facing of fears. Vulnerability. Along the way in our journey, it's important to give these hardships a name. Sometimes it takes acknowledging what we're feeling to allow us to break away, to move on to sunnier days. For example, when I'm having a difficult time, I try and name what it is I'm experiencing. Is it anger? Disappointment? Once I've named it, I allow myself a concrete amount of time to stay in that space. Sometimes that means fifteen minutes to vent to my husband or my best friend, then I try and let it go; I move on. Sometimes it means allowing myself a tearful few moments to acknowledge a disappointment, but then I let that go, too (as best as I can). By doing this, we embrace the idea of the journey and release the friction of the struggle. We acknowledge the stumbles along the way by working with them, rather than against them. It's like a dance that we give ourselves permission to have—one where we gently let the rhythm of our lives come and go, like the tide, swaying with the lessons and truth as we continue to move forward.

There is something very human about acknowledging the messy parts of our creative lives, to feel that for a while, in order to get to the other side, the lightness of life. Still, sometimes it's hard to get through the muck, especially when everything seems to go wrong. We don't get into the craft show we were hoping for. Our magazine submission was rejected. We spill dirty paint water all over our best painting. How can we reframe these creative mishaps for our selves?

In *Traveling Mercies*, Anne Lamott writes about a Buddhist belief—the idea that when several things start going wrong all at once, it is to protect something bigger and greater that is trying to get itself born—and that whatever it is that is trying to come into our world needs for us to be distracted so that it can be born as perfectly as possible. How cool of a concept is this? So, try not and let all the details get to you. Soon you'll be welcoming another idea, another opportunity, another painting or creation that was on its way the whole time.

Whether you're just embarking on your creative journey, or have been on it for years and years, I wish for you this: that you embrace every ebb and flow. That you feel the full breath of inspiration and that it takes you places you won't ever want to leave. That you remember all that you've learned here in this journey we've taken together: to listen to the whispers that are calling you to take notice. To face the direction of your fears and act anyway. To embrace the funky and unique community

that has been waiting for you. To seek ways to find the sacred in the ordinary. To honor all that you were and all that you're becoming. To reveal your truth along the way, even when it hurts. And lastly, that you embrace the journey, complete with all the uncertainties along the way. It will all undoubtedly lead you back to the best parts of your life. Your creativity is your soul rising, your spirit taking flight. Go now. And don't look back.

Opposite page: Journey Toward the Answers, 6" × 12" (15cm × 30cm), mixed media on canvas. *This painting is about how we must live our way, create our way, journey our way to the answers—and how finding our way is often through the creative process rather than reaching a destination.*

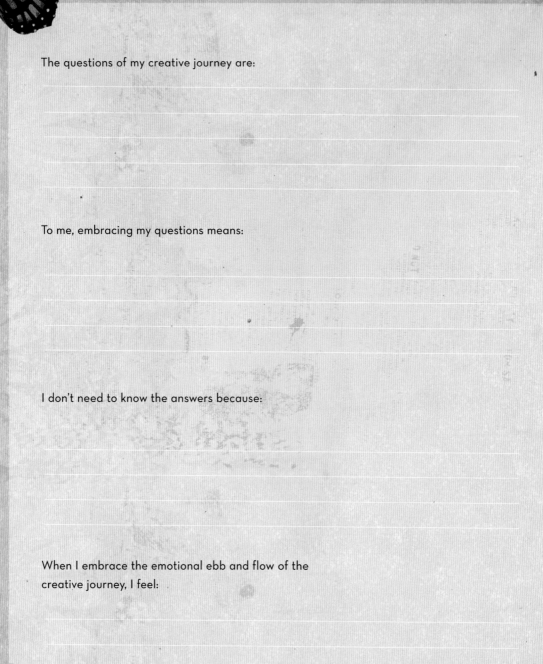

Winged Thoughts

The questions of my creative journey are:

To me, embracing my questions means:

I don't need to know the answers because:

When I embrace the emotional ebb and flow of the creative journey, I feel:

"One must still have chaos in oneself to be able to give birth to a dancing star."
—FRIEDRICH NIETZSCHE

"The important thing is to never stop questioning. Curiosity has its own reason for existing. One cannot but help to be in awe when he contemplates the mysteries of eternity, of life, of the marvelous structure of reality. It is enough if one tries merely to comprehend a little of this mystery everyday. Never lose a holy curiosity."
—ALBERT EINSTEIN

"The great thing in this world is not so much where we stand, as in what direction we are moving." **—OLIVER WENDELL HOLMES**

"There are years that ask questions and years that answer."
—ZORA NEALE HURSTON

"The purpose of art is to lay bare the questions which have been hidden by the answers."
—JAMES ARTHUR BALDWIN

"All changes, even the most longed for, have their melancholy; for what we leave behind us is a part of ourselves. . . ." **—ANATOLE FRANCE**

"Far away in the sunshine are my highest aspirations. I may not reach them, but I can look up and see their beauty, believe in them, and try to follow where they lead."
—LOUISA MAY ALCOTT

"Confidence, like art, never comes from having all the answers; it comes from being open to all the questions." **—EARL GRAY STEVENS**

Embrace the Moment, 7" × 9" (18cm× 23cm) mixed-media encaustic painting on paper by our spirited contributing artist Judy Wise. Judy says this painting "alludes to the beauty inherent in the seemingly ordinary moments of our lives which are never ordinary at all."

Taking Flight with
CONTRIBUTING ARTIST Judy Wise

KRR: Judy, your artistic soul seems to travel well along the creative path. How have you learned to adjust to the inevitable ups and downs of the journey?

JW: I think the first few bumps are the hardest. You know, the first few rejection letters or galleries that don't respond. After that and a bit of careful thought, you realize that it's all part of the drill and something that everyone faces. Even the "overnight" successes have their critics; it's just the way the world is. Most of the time, it isn't directly about you or your art but rather that booth space is limited or a gallery owner has a particular vision that you don't fit into very well. It's more about finding a fit than it is about the validity of your work. All of the work we do has a place in the world. Our challenge is to sift through the opportunities and find our niche.

KRR: Can you share a bit about what the ups and downs have looked like for you?

JW: The hardest thing I've faced is staying motivated in the face of isolation during the months of the year when little is happening (winter!). When I was starting out, the mood swings were extreme, but after many seasons, now I know what to expect. In the summer it is easier to calm myself, while in the winter it is easier to believe that the busy season is just around the corner and that it is important to stay productive. Here in the northern hemisphere, it is particularly difficult for me to adjust to lower levels of light. I have to really push myself on some days to keep all my appointments and promises to myself.

KRR: I can relate to the mood swing thing. I think it has to do with adjusting to the vulnerabilites of beginnings and putting oneself out there. Do you ever struggle with the need to know exactly where it is you're going in your creative endeavors?

JW: I can honestly say that I have always been pretty comfortable not knowing what life would bring me next. I've never had an overall goal or plan, and I still don't. I usually feel like the only thing guiding me is a trust in my own intuition, as though navigating through a thick fog on blind faith. I choose my friends carefully and only surround myself with the kindest, most principled and most loving. I don't know what tomorrow will bring, and I don't worry about it. Sorrow befalls each of us as well as joy. That's what I expect of the future.

KRR: Judy, you are such a beacon to those of us still learning, though I know you believe we never stop learning—which is part of the reason you are so wise! Do you have any suggestions for those who may be facing anxiety about what lies ahead in their creative journeys?

JW: Part of what we're all learning to cope with is the unknown future. We have a choice: We can fear change or we can greet it as we would a thrilling ride at an amusement park. What fascinates me is how things that present themselves as bad luck turn out to be wonderful new opportunities for growth. This happens over and over. Eventually, you realize that there is no good and bad luck. There is only change. What we do with that, whether we embrace it or try to retreat from it, sets a tone for our own failure or success.

KRR: What is the best part of living your creative journey?

JW: Definitely the people I meet along the way. Seeing growth and flowering in the people I meet and in myself. Watching life get smoother and more rewarding as I learn from my work and from my teachers. I believe every person we meet has something to teach us, and I am alert for my lessons. I love partnerships, collaborations, community and a network of helping hands. This is my vision of heaven.

this was a moment

she would never

forget

Learning to Soar

For this project, as with all the others in this book, my goal was to incorporate a couple of this chapter's lovely contributing artist's techniques with my own into a finished work. But as you can see from Judy's artwork on page 116, she uses so many varied techniques that it made it hard to choose just a couple! Ultimately, I decided to try her freehand way of enhancing a painting with journaling and then, once the painting was complete, transform it into an encaustic work.

The term *encaustic* refers to using melted beeswax in a work of art. Prior to this project, I had never made an encaustic painting, but had always wanted to learn—and it was great fun to experiment with! Along the way, you'll also learn some of my favorite ways to create a textured, multilayered background with rubber stamps and to add lines of interest without buying any fancy new tools. So come along with me as we near the end of our journey together with one last project!

MATERIALS FOR CREATING A TEXTURED STAMPED BACKGROUND

7" × 7" (18cm × 18cm) block of wood

3 rubber stamps

heavy-bodied acrylic paints in assorted colors

foam brush

gesso

paper towels

heat gun (optional)

MATERIALS FOR ENCAUSTIC OPAINTING

beeswax

metal stamp

Burnt Umber oil paint

2" (5cm) bristle brush

small potpourri simmer pot, slow cooker or pan and stove

craft knife

rubber glove

heat gun

paper towel

MATERIALS FOR ADDING TEXTURIZED LINES

acrylic paint

old, expired credit card

MATERIALS FOR ENHANCING YOUR PIECE WITH JOURNALING

old book

soft graphite pencil

charcoal pencil (optional)

gel medium

craft knife

119

CREATING A TEXTURED STAMPED BACKGROUND

We'll play around with stamps for this part of the project, giving our background a rich, textured appearance. Be careful, though; using stamps in your paintings can be addictive! It makes it nearly impossible to stop into a craft store without buying a new one every time!

Step 1 ... GESSO WOOD SURFACE

Use a foam brush to gesso the surface of the wood. Allow it to dry all the way. If you wish, you can use a heat gun to speed up the process.

Stretch Your Wings

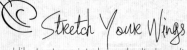

I like to stamp into heavy-bodied acrylics (as opposed to fluid acrylics) because when you stamp into it, the rubber picks up more paint color, allowing for a more dramatic effect.

Step 2 ... PAINT BACKGROUND

Select or mix a shade of heavy-bodied acrylic paint you'd like to use as the primary background color. Use your foam brush to apply a coat of paint to the gessoed surface.

Step 3 ... STAMP DESIGN INTO WET PAINT

While the background paint it still wet, press a stamp firmly into the paint to make an impression. Repeat until you've created a texture you like, and then allow the surface to dry. (Again, you can speed this up with a heat gun if you wish.)

Step 4 ... STAMP ANOTHER DESIGN AND PAINT COLOR

Mix or choose a coordinating color of heavy-bodied acrylic paint. Here I simply added a blue shade to my green background to create a turquoise color in the same palette. Brush the paint directly onto a different rubber stamp, and press it onto your surface to transfer the pattern.

Step 5 ... BLOT EDGES

Use a paper towel to blot the edges and soften the stamp impression. Blot until you've refined the second layer of the background to the level of texture and color you like.

Stretch Your Wings

It's very important to clean acrylic paint off of your stamps immediately with water, or you will ruin your stamp when the paint dries on the rubber.

Step 6 ... ADD A THIRD LAYER OF TEXTURED STAMPING

Select a third stamp, brush some more of the second color of paint onto it and stamp it randomly over the surface to add yet another dimension to the texture. Allow it to dry. Now your beautifully textured, stamped background is ready, and you can go on to paint the subject of your choice.

ADDING TEXTURIZED LINES

Adding textured lines to your painting can be as simple as swiping an old credit card through paint and then sliding it across your surface.

Step 7 ... ADD PAINT WITH CREDIT CARD

After you've painted your subject matter, load the edge of a credit card with paint, and use it to add lines of texture to the surface of your background. You can apply different amounts of paint and pressure to make pencil-thin lines or heavy lines, depending on your preference.

ENHANCING YOUR PIECE WITH JOURNALING
{ Contributing Artist's Technique by Judy Wise }

I often cut and paste words onto my painted collages, but I enjoyed setting aside my inhibitions and actually writing my words directly into the surface in this part of the painting, thanks to Judy's inspiration.

Step 8 ... WRITE WITH PENCIL OVER DRY BACKGROUND

Journal on the background with a soft graphite pencil. It can be as neat or as messy as you like, as readable or illegible.

Step 9 ... BLEND GRAPHITE AND ADD COLLAGE WORDS

Use your finger to blend the graphite and soften it. Again, you can leave it as clear as you want, or make it almost illegible. Use a craft knife to cut any words that strike you as significant from an old book. This is another way to enhance the meaning of your work. Here I selected "This was a moment she would never forget." Use gel medium to adhere them to your subject. If you'd like, you can use a charcoal pencil to trace around the edges and enhance your cut-out words.

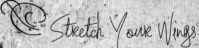

Stretch Your Wings

If you'd like, you can repeat the stamping techniques used earlier as a top layer, as I did here. Try using white paint—it can brighten up an entire piece.

ENCAUSTIC PAINTING
{ Contributing Artist's Technique by Judy Wise }

Next, we'll both be learning something new as we turn our ordinary piece into an encaustic painting following Judy's tips. This was new for me, but I so enjoyed the process of discovering what beeswax can do! And happily, I found that it's very forgiving when you make mistakes—just reheat and redo.

Step 10 ... BRUSH BEESWAX ONTO SURFACE

Melt beeswax in a small potpourri simmer pot, in a slow cooker or on the stove. (The recommended temperature is 225 degrees Fahrenheit [107 degrees Celsius].) Use a 2" (5cm) bristle brush to apply a layer of wax over the surface of the piece.

Step 11 ... SMOOTH BRUSH MARKS WITH HEAT

Use a heat gun to melt the brush marks into a smooth, matte surface.

Step 12 ... STAMP IMPRESSION INTO COOLING WAX

Let the wax set until it's no longer hot but not yet cold. Use a metal stamp or object to make impressions in the drying wax surface.

Step 13 ... CUT DETAIL LINES INTO WAX

Use a craft knife to carve small lines into the wax in areas that you think could use more definition or texture.

Step 14 ... APPLY PAINT TO STAMPED AND CARVED AREAS

Take a bit of Burnt Umber oil paint (a great color for distressing) and use your fingers to rub it thoroughly into the impressions you made with the stamp and the knife.

Stretch Your Wings

Buff the surface of your encaustic work every few months to restore the satiny surface. With regular maintenance, eventually the wax will stop "blooming" and stay satiny in appearance.

Step 15 ... RUB PAINT FROM SURFACE

Using a paper towel, rub the excess oil paint off of the surface, leaving only the distressed, inked impression behind.

Step 16 ... BUFF WAX

Put an ordinary rubber glove on your hand and give it some time to warm a bit to the heat of your hand. Use the side of your warm, gloved hand to buff the surface of the wax until the finish has a sheen to it.

Resources: Places to Fly

ONLINE CREATIVE RESOURCES

Another Girl at Play (http://another girlatplay.com): A place where female artists and business owners share their experiences, stories and wisdom. This site is hugely inspirational to me.

Blogger (www.blogger.com): A place where you can start your own blog, for free! Follow the online directions, and off you go.

Flickr (www.flickr.com): A photo-sharing Web site that hosts countless art and craft groups. Participants can upload a photo of their latest art project to a specific group, such as the "mixed-media painting group" or the "vintage-inspired jewelry group," then participate in giving and receiving feedback or in discussions on various topics within the group. This site is known for being innovative and easy to use—and for pushing the boundaries of creative photo sharing.

Get Crafty (www.getcrafty.com): A wonderful site full of crafty goodness, projects, photos and forums.

Illustration Friday (www.illustration friday.com): A great destination for a weekly illustration challenge, with an active forum meant specifically to build creative community. You can ask questions, receive feedback, find local crafters in your area and more.

Inspire Me Thursday (www.inspire methursday.com): A weekly dose of inspiration that will have you wanting to dive right into the creative challenges and connect with other participants. This site also has a healthy dose of inspiring quotes, recommended books and links. One of the first online communities I joined, Inspire Me Thursday had my art and my spirit growing with meaning each week. It's a wonderful starting point for anybody looking for community, no matter where you are in your creative path.

MyCraftivity (www.mycraftivity.com): An online craft community similar to Facebook or MySpace, except it's created exclusively for crafters of all types (including scrapbooking, jewelry, knitting, collage, and more). Members create their own pages, connect with other crafters through comments and forums, and even blog about their latest creations.

Photobooth Friday (www.flickr.com/ groups/photoboothfriday): Fun monthly challenges that will have you joyously running to the nearest photobooth!

Self-Portrait Challenge (www.self portraitchallenge.net): An online community encouraging self-expression with weekly themed self-portraiture challenges. You'd be surprised how participating in something you might otherwise not do pushes your growth in your creative path. I love how this Web site feels inclusive. You don't have to be a skilled photographer to participate. It's quirky. And fun. And honest.

Shutter Sisters (http://shuttersisters. com): A collaborative photo blog welcoming all women with a passion for photography, from experts to amateurs alike. Visit for weekly, sometimes daily challenges and ideas to get your inner photographer out to play!

Sparkletopia (http://sparkletopia. squarespace.com): Filled with overflowing inspiration throughout the day, including musings, links, sparkling stories to inspire you and more. This site was the brainchild of one of this book's contributing artists, Christine Mason Miller, and I absolutely love it—a daily read for sure.

Sunday Scribblings (www.sunday scribblings.blogspot.com): A weekly dose of writing prompts to inspire and motivate you to write.

Whip Up (http://whipup.net): Full of eye candy, crafty challenges, ideas, helpful tips and a very active community forum. This site is wonderful to visit for inspiration.

Yahoo Groups (www.groups.yahoo. com): A place to search and find a seemingly unending source of creative groups, including everything from stamping to papier mâché to quilting to mixed media and more. These groups act as forums—one long discussion on various topics within each one. Explore. Enjoy. Participate!

SUPPLIES

Archiver's (www.archiversonline.com):
A huge selection of scrapbooking papers and supplies. If you're lucky, there is a store near you, but if not, the online store is a good alternative.

Character Constructions (www.characterconstructions.com): Full of wonderfully unique and whimsical stamps, both mounted and unmounted. Contributing artist Laurie Mika suggested I use this source for stamps for creating the polymer clay dress form on pages 40–41, and I'm so glad I did.

Zettiology (www.teeshamoore.com): Great selection of whimsical stamps, stencils and inspiration.

SMALL BUSINESS SUPPORT

Etsy (www.etsy.com): A popular site where you can sell your handcrafted goods.

Constant Contact (www.constantcontact.com): A great way to send newsletters to your growing listserve.

The Switchboards (www.theswitchboards.com): An online forum of creative business women sharing their secrets and insights.

Paypal (www.paypal.com): A secure, easy way to receive payment online.

Vista Print (www.vistaprint.com): For all your business card, stationery and other promotional needs.

ART RETREATS

Art and Soul (www.artandsoulretreat.com): A paper, fabric, jewelry and fiber arts retreat held in cities nationwide and internationally throughout the year. I've been to the Portland, Oregon, retreat, and I found it to be a rewarding experience filled with fantastic workshops.

ArtFest (www.teeshamoore.com): A one-of-a-kind mixed-media retreat held in Port Townsend, Washington, once a year. This camp-like retreat is an experience you don't want to miss. It was at ArtFest that my creative journey took off.

Art FiberFest: (www.teeshamoore.com): This smaller sister of ArtFest focuses on fiber arts.

The Art Nest (www.theartnest.net): A mixed-media retreat, held in a gorgeous mountain cabin in Park City, Utah.

The Artists' Nook (www.theartistsnook.net): This Fort Collins, Colorado, art boutique offers year-round workshops for mixed-media, altered book, altered art and rubber stamp enthusiasts.

Art Unraveled (www.artunraveled.com): A mixed-media art retreat held every summer in Phoenix, Arizona.

Valley Ridge (www.valleyridgeartstudio.com): A Muscoda, Wisconsin, art retreat that offers weekend workshops throughout the year. Emphasis is on book art, metals, mixed media and fiber arts.

CRAFTY MAGAZINES

Cloth Paper Scissors **(www.quiltingarts.com):** This is a great magazine full of art projects and tips for all levels, from beginners to advanced. I love this magazine because it features a very true variety of all art forms: collage, quilting, painting, assemblage, jewelry, doll making and on and on.

Somerset Studio **(www.stampington.com):** I remember when I first stumbled upon this magazine. I was totally mesmerized by all the inspiring projects. With a focus on paper crafts and stamping, this magazine not only gives how-to's but also does a great job of writing artist profiles.

Index

Stretch Your Creative Wings with These Inspiring Titles from North Light Books

LIVING THE CREATIVE LIFE

Ricë Freeman-Zachery

What is creativity anyway? Where do ideas come from? How do successful artists get started? How do you know when a piece is finished? Inside *Living the Creative Life*, you'll find answers to these questions and more ideas and insights from 15 successful artists in a variety of mediums—from assemblage to fiber arts, beading to mixed-media collage.
ISBN-10: 1-58180-994-8, ISBN-13: 978-1-58180-994-7, paperback, 144 pages, Z0949

THE ART OF PERSONAL IMAGERY

Corey Moortgat

This book introduces a new approach to collage, blending traditional collage techniques with methods of chronicling life events. The result is innovative, fresh and meaningful art that uses modern photos, vintage images and personal writing to commemorate everything from special occasions to extraordinary everydays. With step-by-step instructions and photos for countless techniques and 9 intensive projects, you'll learn to achieve your own trademark style.
ISBN-10: 1-58180-990-5, ISBN-13: 978-1-58180-990-9, paperback, 128 pages, Z0937

KALEIDOSCOPE

Suzanne Simanaitis

Kaleidoscope delivers your creative muse directly to your workspace. Featuring interactive and energizing creativity prompts ranging from inspiring stories to personality tests, doodle exercises and a cut-and-fold shrine, this is one-stop shopping for getting your creative juices flowing. The book showcases eye candy artwork and projects with instruction from some of the hottest collage, mixed-media and altered artists on the zine scene today.
ISBN-10: 1-58180-879-8 ISBN-13: 978-1-58180-879-7, paperback, 144 pages, Z0346

WIDE OPEN

Randi Feuerhelm-Watts

Open yourself up to a whole new way of looking at yourself, your world and your art journal. The *Wide Open* book and deck set is all about challenging yourself to take your art to the next level. The set includes 50 idea cards featuring mixed-media artist Randi Feuerhelm-Watts's art on one side and thought-provoking instruction on the other, plus a journal for recording your ideas and artwork.
ISBN-10: 1-58180-911-5, ISBN-13: 978-1-58180-911-4, 64 pages with accompanying cards, Z0653

These and other fine North Light Books are available at your local craft retailer, bookstore or online supplier, or visit our Web site at www.mycraftivity.com.